FIVE CENTURIES OF
ITALIAN MAJOLICA

Bowl decorated with grotesques, dedicated to Pope Julius II. Casteldurante, Zoan Maria Vasaro (1508)
New York, Metropolitan Museum of Art (Lehman Coll.)

FIVE CENTURIES OF
ITALIAN MAJOLICA

BY GIUSEPPE LIVERANI

McGRAW-HILL BOOK COMPANY, INC., 1960
NEW YORK - TORONTO - LONDON

Original title:

La maiolica italiana sino alla comparsa della porcellana europea

Electa Editrice, Milan, 1958

© 1960 by Electa Editrice S.p.A.

Library of Congress Catalog Card Number: 59-13206

Printed in Italy

38129

TO THE MEMORY OF MY PARENTS
AND OF MY TEACHER, GAETANO BALLARDINI

CONTENTS

i TYPICAL SHAPES OF PHARMACY VASES. FAENZA (EARLY 17TH CENT.). FAENZA MUSEUM.

*Ceramics:
definition;
classification*

To facilitate the understanding of much that follows it will be useful to keep in mind that everything which man fashions out of clay and then fires is a ceramic product. As much because of the abundance of the raw material and ease in procuring it as because of its extreme plasticity and its property of retaining shape when dried (and even more when fired), ceramic products were among the first and the most common that man formed on the slow journey toward civilization.

What happens to clay when it is subjected to fire should be mentioned. Owing to the nature of the principal component and the action of the ingredients added, the body of the ceramic object assumes, after firing, different aspects in structure and color, becoming either porous or dense, white or colored.

These peculiarities make it possible to distinguish certain groups: *terracotta*, with a colored, porous body; *earthenware*, with a white or cream-colored, porous body; *stoneware*, with a colored, dense (or nonporous) body; and *porcelain*, with a white, dense body. From these groups come minor categories with characteristics that can be differentiated further, but all can be placed in one or another of the major groups.

A subgroup that, because of its immense diffusion over a long period, may be considered one of the principal groups is *faïence*, which is terracotta with a vitreous coating, either transparent (glaze) or opaque (enamel).

For practical purposes, in fact, a porous vessel of terracotta is scarcely usable without eliminating the porosity. This was achieved first in prehistoric times by polishing or burnishing, later, in Greece and Rome, by the application of an argillaceous coating, and then in the Middle East by a vitreous silicoalkaline glaze or by a lead glaze. The latter, originating in Egypt, Mesopotamia, and Persia, spread to Rome, Byzantium, and the Islamic world, and was almost the exclusive covering for ceramic vessels in all European countries from the Middle Ages until the beginning of the eighteenth century when, with Böttger's discovery of porcelain, the exotic, long-sought-for Chinese product joined it. In the course of the same century, from Rhenish origins in stoneware—dense, with a silicoalkaline coating that was a revival of the coating of classical tradition—came the last of the ceramic families, earthenware, beginning in England and spreading rapidly all over.

It must also be remembered that, because of the same need for color to which we owe painted ornamentation, it was customary, from the late Roman and Byzantine times onward, to use together with the glaze a white clay coating, or "slip" (ingobbio), already known to the Attic potters and their predecessors. This slip not only enhanced the transparency of the glaze but also offered an ideal ground for the chromatic and tonal harmonies of the decoration. Moreover, scratching the slip (sgraffito process) exposed the reddish-brown body beneath and thus provided a contrast that enlivened a linear design.

Faïence, then, may be of three kinds: glazed, coated with slip before glazing, or enameled (majolica). In comparatively recent times faïence has embodied the richest and most widely spread tradition of pottery, in Italy as in other countries.

The history of ceramics is a long one. The first concern of the art was with one of man's fundamental needs—the collecting and storing of liquids. Ceramics may therefore be classed among the primeval arts, appearing suddenly, in the Neolithic period, when man first became distinguishable from brute. The advantages and special qualities of clay made it, almost spontaneously, all over the world, the material of utensils precious for the purpose of primitive man. It was abundant and accessible to all; it was easy to shape—so easy that the work was apparently left to women and children, the men being engaged in hunting. Objects shaped from clay, after drying and hardening in the sun or in the embers of a fire, would hold their shape. They became substitutes for receptacles of wood, bone, or stone. Originally, primitive man sought, by polishing the clay object, only to diminish its porosity; later he sought to embellish it and to endow it with a religious or symbolic character by adorning it with incisions or with designs in relief. Evidently he was inspired by the other great primitive arts of braiding and weaving, or was consciously or unconsciously influenced by suggestions from the world of nature.

The next step, when painting became one of the ornamental devices, is approximately contemporaneous with the discovery of metals. The simplest structural forms were used: the basin, cylinder, or bell shape, generally round in horizontal cross section, but sometimes square at the mouth; the vertical line was sometimes more complex, with or without handles added. All these forms became more elaborate after the invention of the potter's wheel, which gave the craftsman enormous scope. Painted decoration and the firing process were developed and perfected at the same time.

From the beginning, the aesthetic element of the shape seems to have been bound up with the functional character of the receptacle. This is shown by the tradition closely observed by particular ethnic-regional groups. In ornamentation the evolution is less straightforward, with instinct, the influences of nature, and magic impulses all playing their part. The representation of things—plants, animals, persons, and stellar bodies—proceeds side by side, or alternates, or mingles with abstract and geometric fantasies.

Contacts between the great civilizations of the Eastern Mediterranean and of the Near East were frequent in the early ages of our history and can be proved to have existed also in prehistoric times, but they did not lead to a fusion of the two types of pottery. In Greece, on the one hand, the local clay paste and the logical character of the Western mind led to forms ever more clearly defined and consistent, with a strict adherence to functional values and obedience to clear architectonic laws. In Egypt, Mesopotamia, and

Persia, on the other hand, a dreamier temperament and the gradual but steady increase in the use of siliceous compounds, owing to the nature of the soil, led to shapes of softer outline, less rigidly geometric, and, because of the qualities of the materials used, to the early discovery of a glaze coating that acted as a unifying element while eliminating the porosity of the paste.

The argillaceous coating which was used to eliminate porosity in what is generally called classical pottery—Greek, Hellenistic, and Roman—did not lend itself to painted decoration. Nor in fact was painted decoration desired, as we see by the Attic potters' abandonment of the faint polychromy of orientalized and Ionic ceramics and their turning to refined anthropomorphous representation in black and red. Such representation conceded nothing to pictorialism; there was no intention of suggesting three-dimensional planes, which might have lessened perception of the purely volumetric values of the vase.

Eastern pottery expresses a different taste. The Eastern potters' sensual attraction to color was encouraged by the vitreous, flowing quality of the glaze, which gave brilliant tones—dark blue, turquoise, green, yellow, purple, and white—to the metal oxides.

The two methods of work were consolidated during the Hellenistic age, when we find products with an argillaceous ground and a vitreous glaze. The new style spread rapidly from Alexandria and the countries of the Middle East to Asia, as far as the China of the Han dynasty, and to Europe, to the lands under Roman domination. In the dark-green or tawny ferruginous yellow glaze, lead now became the chief element of fusion.

In the red glazed pottery of Arezzo the Romans, with the help of Greek artisans, had already achieved a type of refined craftsmanship that could rival vessels cast in precious metals; now they produced the new kind of pottery also. The gradual deterioration of form in sculpture, which was reflected in ceramic ornamentation, emphasized the utilitarian element. The vitreous glaze made dishes and ewers more solid and durable. By the time the Empire fell this glaze was known all over the West.

Preserving the tradition of Rome, but under the influence of Oriental form and color, Byzantium developed this style of ceramic art, enriched particularly by the Egyptian contribution, at least until the time of the split which occurred after the Council of Chalcedon, and even for some time later. The appearance of tableware made from semiprecious stones and metals, the decoration of walls with a mosaic of painted panels instead of costly enamel tiles—possibly in imitation of the by then remote Assyrian, Babylonian, and Persian monuments—brought the Byzantine craftsmen much nearer to the creation of a new type of ceramic ware: vessels with plastic ornamentation in imitation of metal *repoussé* decoration, and covered with a monochrome green or tawny yellow glaze; others with glazes stained to imitate semiprecious stones; still others with the addition of color in the veining of the glaze or with decorative patterns in the manner of engraved silver, incised on the white slip beneath a transparent glaze; and finally, vessels with painted designs sometimes enclosed within an outlined panel. We find these styles, especially the last, mentioned in the *Didascalia* of Heraclius and Theophilus.

The rise and triumph of the Islamic world gave renewed vitality to Middle Eastern ceramic art and restored to it a unity of inspiration beyond regional diversities. At the same time there was an increase in the flow of reciprocal influences between the lands of the Middle East and those of the neighboring Byzantine Empire and the Far East.

Various expressions of the potter's art appear in every region of that vast politico-religious empire and in these other lands. We find transparent and opaque glazes over siliceous or argillaceous paste; ornamentation incised in siliceous pastes, with resulting patches or planes in *sopraccolore* under the transparent glaze; decoration scratched on the slip to expose the reddish clay below; polychrome decorations painted on white enamel or ivory-colored, dark-blue, or turquoise enamel; and decorations painted under an intensely pellucid glaze, which give the impression of designs seen through deep water. We find dense white clays and the iridescent hues of the metallic lusterware that was imported from the East into Spain, along the southern coasts of the Mediterranean. The Mohammedan, with his love of sumptuous adornment, with his whimsical and lively imagination, stimulated by the limits imposed upon his representation of figures, and influenced by the use of precious-metal vessels, concentrated all the fervor of his art on ceramics. He used them to serve a variety of purposes, in the field of architecture as much as for table and domestic utensils, and he endowed the art with prodigious vitality.

Contacts with the Western world, through cultural, political, and commercial exchanges, through the Crusades, and through piratical enterprise, all made their contributions to the art. Sicily, a country which was under the direct rule of Islam and therefore had her part to play in Islamic life (as is still evident in her architectural monuments), may have been the connecting bridge to the southern regions of Italy, formerly most susceptible to Byzantine influence. But the Islamic influence also reached Northern Italy and the large island of Sardinia. Circular ceramic plaques used as architectural adornments, pavements, wall mosaics, and certain thematic decorative designs are evidence of this.

The rest of Europe—with the exception of Mohammedan Spain—seemed, in the field of ceramics, to depend upon the now languishing classical tradition, upheld only by the sturdily tenacious conservatism of the ordinary people, whose artistic taste developed as the classical tradition declined. In Italy these contacts, and a still more lively tradition of classical culture, revitalized ancient memories of the craft and caused it, at the close of the tenth century and for a short time after, to flourish anew.

From what we have already seen it seems clear that, even if the wonderful development of ceramic art in the countries of Islamic culture exerted an influence over the evolution—or rather the transformation—of the Italian style, the strength of this style derived from the still-vital local tradition of classical origin, a tradition which showed no signs of disappearing.

Continuity of tradition is proved by the discovery, in various parts of Italy, of vessels all dating from the late Middle Ages, coated with a vitreous lead glaze of a dark-green or tawny yellow color. We have already mentioned this pottery as the last achievement of the Roman potter of the Augustan age. The most convincing finds are from Ostia, the port of Rome, from the Roman Forum itself, from the excavations of Fonte di Juthurna, and from Sardinia. Near Tharros, in the Gulf of Oristano, vases discovered in a Christian tomb, together with coins of Justinian and Heraclius, can be ascribed with certainty to the seventh century; relics excavated in the Forum are probably of the ninth century.

The numerous examples of pottery from the Roman Forum—nearly all jars and most of them unearthed as whole pieces—testify to an equilibrium of form and a conservatism of ornamental styles and technical process that assign them to the golden age of classical ceramics. We find jars of pure ovoid form, without a foot, sometimes with swelling shoulders, decorated with smooth horizontal reeding in parallel rings around the cylindrical neck; they are finished with a robust vertical handle attached at a right angle and balanced on the opposite side by a short cylindrical spout inserted in the upper part of the belly, or by a flattened elliptical spout, sometimes inserted in the neck. These jars are ornamented with bosses in the form of rosettes or, more often, bosses flattened like scales, generally arranged in vertical rows of tongues which, pointing upward, divide the oval shape into segments and thus accentuate the vertical line. Sometimes the scales are distributed FIG. *iii*

12

haphazardly, or overlapping one another, to give the impression of a ripe pine cone.

The equilibrium of the various parts, controlled by strict geometric principles, the symmetry, the sense of volume, the surfaces enriched but not broken by the narrow ornamental ribbing, the monochrome glaze, often of a dark hue which does not distract the eye with colors or reflections but emphasizes the rounded lines—all these qualities make some of the vessels perfect specimens of abstract plastic art. In others, a more complicated shape is smothered in the play of light and shadow on the overlapping scales, which frequently give the impression of a fruit. In still others, the extreme sinuosity of the form is emphasized by a long spout.

It is form, pure form, which emerges in this incubatory period of Italian ceramics, the paleo-Italian period, dominated by a preeminently plastic conception. In later expressions this plastic-volumetric sense sometimes gave way to the complementary elements of line and color and eventually produced hybrid forms of art. Nevertheless, the sense of pure form in ceramic objects was preserved for many centuries in the humblest vessels in use by the common people, who were less susceptible to the lure of painted ornamentation.

The continuity of ceramic tradition in Italy is also proved by the glazing processes; gradually the transparent colored glaze used in Roman times was supplanted by the opaque glaze of the late Middle Ages. It is precisely the gradual pace of this evolution which counsels caution in estimating the influence of Middle Eastern lands in promoting the adoption of the opaque glaze. Indeed, the method of rendering the glaze opaque, or better, of producing a white glaze, was known to the Roman potters, even if, in the turbulent centuries that followed the fall of the Empire, the process does not seem to have had a wide practical application.

Basins in architecture

The Eastern contribution is more obvious in the development from plastic to pictorial colored ornamentation, examples of which

ii FAÇADE WITH NICHES FOR ORNAMENTAL BASINS. PAVIA, CHURCH OF S. MICHELE MAGGIORE.

are found in the large circular plaques or basins that Romanesque builders inserted in the walls of public, and especially of religious, edifices. The Eastern influence also made itself felt through Sicily and the regions of Southern Italy, which served as intermediaries.

The use, from the first centuries of the Christian era, of smooth concave bowls or basins for the adornment of outer walls is documented by the excavations at Ostia. Perhaps ceramic bowls fulfilled in less important buildings the function of circular disks of colored marble in more noble edifices; later on, in regions bordering on the Byzantine Empire and even further afield (for example, in Bulgaria), small ceramic tablets replaced the costly and complex wall mosaics of vitreous paste.

The persistence of this style in the Byzantine Era is shown in the architectonic details of the apse of the Church of S. Vitale in Ravenna. In the mosaic of the Court of Theodora we see a clear example of glazed disks set into the ornamentation above the capitals to reflect light.

The most widespread application of this method of ornamentation is, however, found in the eleventh and succeeding centuries, when

13

FIG. *ii*

a renewed fervor of construction, which resulted from the reorganization of civic, political, and economic life in the free communes and in the Italian seafaring republics, was everywhere raising solemn and magnificent buildings to serve the functions of the community and to satisfy the religious aspirations of the people.

The austere, robust style of these buildings was softened externally by ornamentation arising from the structural elements themselves, which were of classical derivation; variations in style were the product of regional differences and reflected the influence of workmen near and far—from beyond the Alps and even from beyond the sea. Embellishment was due to the renewed taste for color, which expressed itself in the materials offered locally—in marble, terracotta, and faïence, glazed or enameled.

Lombardy (Pavia), Emilia (Parma, Bologna, Ravenna, Faenza), Tuscany (Pisa, Lucca), Sardinia, the Marches (Ascoli, Ancona, Tolentino), Latium (Rome), and still other regions, though in lesser measure, show a wealth of buildings dating from the end of the eleventh and the whole of the twelfth and thirteenth centuries. In that period ceramic art was adopted as a decorative element, as seen in the use of disks or basins generally placed so as to underline architectural planes or to accentuate arcading below the cornices. Churches, and particularly bell towers, were the structures most commonly enriched with ceramic ornamentation, a fact which has led observers to suppose that the architect did not merely want to add a new note of color to break the monotony of brick or stone, but that he had also the intention of making a votive offering or of preserving trophies. The supposition is supported by the absence of these decorative disks or basins in the interior of the edifice, a consecrated place where the works of infidels might not have been well received.

We have mentioned trophies or votive offerings. In fact, a great number of the basins reveal an exotic origin, and we may presume that they were the trophies not only of peaceful commercial exchanges but also of bitter strife: warfare, invasions, depredations, or piracies. They may have been also memorials of pilgrimages which involved, beyond the dangers incurred, vows and propitiatory or grateful offerings. These basins were probably inspired, as we have said, by disks of colored marble, and they added a colorful note to the adornment of the building. The singularly monochrome touches of color, white, green, tawny yellow, or purple—which we frequently find in the simplest products of local skill, such as enameled tiles or bowls—are enriched with designs in polychrome or in iridescent metallic luster when they come from the lands of the Middle East, whether Byzantine or Mohammedan, from North Africa, Spain, or perhaps even from Sicily.

The faithful could admire on the walls of their churches glazed basins with thin yellowish or rose-red lines scratched in the white clay of the slip or half hidden by the monochrome colored glaze; paintings in black under a thicker and more flowing glaze; enamels superimposed and juxtaposed according to more or less clearly defined patterns and covering partially or wholly the colored clay body of the basin; white backgrounds on which stood out, colored or painted with golden luster, vivid forms and figures evocative of a remote and fabulous world and arousing nebulous dreams and desires. It was inevitable that the potter should have responded to the spell of this new art.

The attraction exercised by imported colored products is reflected as much in ceramic receptacles as in pavement tiles, and possibly in the designs of these tiles the decorators were much influenced also by the design of stained-glass windows. The strong uniform dark outline which delineates the figures, and separates their green filling from the white background, may in fact be related to the hard line of the lead strips which hold together the panes of variously colored glass. Examples

Archaic period: S. Italy; Umbro-Latian, Tuscan, Romagnese group

of tiles so influenced are to be found even in Northern Europe, particularly in Germany, where the art of stained glass flowered in the tenth and eleventh centuries. In the old Cathedral of Hamburg may be seen the surviving tiles of the cenotaph erected between 1320 and 1330 to Pope Benedict V. In the Abbey of St. Paul and in the Cathedral of Utrecht in the Netherlands, the pavement of the second half of the fourteenth century, with figures and ornamental designs painted in brown, green, and yellow on a white background, is quite different from the usual ornamental mosaics. Other examples from the same century are to be found in Burgundy, France, and Spain.

In Italy also this affinity of decorative design can be seen. At Assisi, in the Upper Church, where in the middle of the thirteenth century the first polychrome window glass appeared—the work of masters from beyond the Alps—we can see tiles with green leaves outlined in black on a white ground, on the steps of the altar, and other tiles adorned with geometric designs of alternating white and green grounds. At Orvieto, in 1321, the potters prepared enameled tiles to complete the mosaics of the façade of the Cathedral.

Undoubtedly a much more widespread use of painted decoration is found in tableware and in the receptacles used in pharmacies.

The vessels of the archaic period, although enriched with color, remained strictly subject to exigencies of a practical order; and, as in Ancient Greece, the shape of containers and their complements—handles, spout, foot, etc.— were determined by considerations of utility. The forms were "hollow" or "flat," as Piccolpasso was later to call them. By "hollow" he meant a form enclosing an empty space and therefore developing either along mainly vertical lines or more widely open, with more or less broad sides widening upward; by "flat" he meant a horizontal extension forming a surface on which food could be placed. Whether hollow or flat, vessels and dishes were turned on the potter's wheel and had a cir-

cular section, even when the rims, in imitation of vessels wrought in metal, were decorated with lobes impressed upon the soft paste, or with applied fringes, or other ornaments. The plastic sense expressed schematically in the simple forms is not lost in the painted decoration, and the consistency with which the forms are maintained shows how closely they conformed to need.

The study of form and decoration, as well as techniques, leads to the identification of characteristic local styles that had a more or less wide area of influence. Although investigation has not yet uncovered all the links of the chain that may have connected the South with the towns of Central and Northern Italy, intensified research in the archives and increased attention to archaeological findings from the Middle Ages and later periods have made plain enough during the last decades the role that Sicily and the other regions of the Mediterranean must have played during the archaic period of Italian majolica.

The most important links, first with the Byzantine Empire and later with the Islamic world, are reflected in the ceramics unearthed in Sicily, Apulia, and Calabria. These ceramics FIG. iv are painted in brown and green, and occasionally in pale yellow, either directly on a straw-colored clay body or on an intermediate coating of slip or rudimentary enamel under a transparent glaze. Occasionally a more developed sense of color is seen in the use of a brick red or, more rarely, of a dark blue, together with ferruginous brown, green, and yellow, on fragments most frequently found, so far, in Apulia.

Many of these ceramics exhibit such close affinity to the basins in the external walls of buildings in Northern Italy as to raise the question: How many of these relics came, along with those from Middle Eastern countries, from the southern regions of Italy and from Sicily? Even now, while we wait for the fuller information that wider research and a more careful examination of what has already been discovered will provide, we perceive a continuity, a characteristic nobility, in the work of the Norman, the Swabian, and the Aragonese periods. Our knowledge of the work of Central and Northern Italy is much more detailed and permits us to single out three broad regional groups whose areas of influence, radiating from local centers, may be said to cover the whole of the central and northern part of the peninsula.

PLS. I, 2

To the south of the Apennines, on the Tyrrhenian side, we find the Umbro-Latian group, with Orvieto as its center, and the Tuscan group, with its center at Montalcino, near Siena; in the north, on the Adriatic side, is the group of the Romagna, with its center at Faenza and its area of influence the Marches and the Veneto. The factor common to all the groups—a factor that the Italian centers share with the Mediterranean countries—is the palette: dominant green with brown on a clear background; more rarely, dark blue is included, and occasionally yellow, often the result of impurities. The distinguishing factor is the form of the hollow receptacles.

PL. 3

Orvieto, through the wealth of findings from quarries and wells and through the data in its archives, may be said to represent ceramic art in the zone roughly contained within the confines of Umbria and Latium. In the latter region, which includes Rome, the attention paid to the art of the Imperial age, and of the ages immediately before and after, has perhaps led to the neglect of evidence of less fortunate periods. In any event, the classical forms in Italian art are those whose evolution can be followed most closely.

The water vase, ovoid, footless, with a cylindrical neck, a funnel-shaped or sometimes elliptical spout, and a more or less wide, vertical handle, has been known at least since the paleo-Italian period. This shape is repeated in the *panata*, footless, with a more or less barrel-shaped body, a straight neck, a vertical, wide strap handle, and an applied spout like a flattened funnel, occasionally extending into a long beak. The usually flowing lines of the shape sometimes stiffen into sharply defined angles and planes, betraying the influence of the new technique of metalwork.

Another shape—this one not hollow—which comes down to us from classical times is the *tazzotto*, a plate with a vertical rim, which swells out toward the base and is decorated with a border of little tongues—a shape repeated without much variation. Also classical in origin is the basin with a lobed rim, which looks rather like a rosette, the inspiration apparently coming from a model in metal.

Closely related to the spouted water pitcher, or *panata*, is the jug, which has two characteristic shapes in Orvieto. One type of jug is footless and globular, with the body resting on a light pad. This shape, clearly descended from the Greek oenochoë, is found also in the Romagna area, especially around the fifteenth century. The other type, extended vertically and twice as high as it is wide, is a shape found also in the Tuscan workshops. From the broadly spreading foot the pear-shaped body rises without closing in very much. It terminates in a mouth with a three-lobed spout, like a nose turned upside down, which is formed by bending the rim cleverly at the top. This spout is balanced on the opposite side by a sturdy cordlike handle. What these jugs lose in volumetric unity they gain in elegance. In the jug is manifested very clearly a taste for vibrant, sensitive Gothic line, and both forms seem to belong to a later period.

In the Romagna, on the Adriatic side, the globular jug, wide in the middle, and the footed jug were preceded by another more rigid, cylindrical shape contracted slightly at the base and at the mouth, which gave life to the form without losing the air of solidity. In some cases the middle section, or belly, between the two places where it narrows, tends to assume the shape of two opposed truncated cones, with a clearly marked line of conjunction. This peculiarity is noticeable especially in centers situated at the far end of the zone, near the seacoast, at Ravenna, Rimini, and Fano. Here also the proportions of height to width, which are usually one to one and a half, may increase to a ratio of one to two, sometimes accompanied by a noticeably accentuated contraction above and below.

In ornamentation the sense of color had by this time almost completely taken the place of the plastic sense; when plasticity is encountered, it is emphasized by the use of color. This is found only in a few vessels, PL. 4 jugs, and two-handled jars of Orvietan workmanship, with designs in relief of twigs bearing pine cones, sometimes with a bust, or armorial bearings, or a heraldic device in the central branch. This type of heraldic design apparently derives from an esoteric religious tradition, which may be of Etruscan origin.

The *vasa medicinalia*, recorded in Siena in 1202, reveal the contribution of the pharmacy to the repertory of vase forms from the archaic period on. The globular footless water jars, with a stirrup handle on each side of the cylindrical neck, which rises straight from the round shoulders (mentioned in connection with the Orvietan plastic ornamentation in relief), may be considered as vessels for either household or pharmacy use. The *albarello*, or drugpot, on the other hand, with its cylindrical body contracted at the waist and its similar close contraction and projecting outer rim at the mouth and foot, is reserved strictly for pharmaceutical use. It originated in containers of bamboo, made by cutting the canes at the nodes and closing the sections above and below with membranes tied at the point where the nodes protrude. In these containers spices and other products of the exotic flora of the Near and Middle East were transported to the West. When they reached our shores, their wood wrappings were replaced by terracotta vases, whose shapes were inspired by the original bamboo receptacles. The very word *albarello*, from the Arabic *el barani*, proves this derivation. The form was rare at first, but it soon gained favor and with extraordinary rapidity became widespread; varying slightly in form to accord

with varying functions, it has persisted down to our times as a typical pharmaceutical vessel, being used not only for spices and drugs but also for unguents and other compounds.

The exigencies of color, as we have already noted, led to the adoption of the white ground in pottery. That the white ground itself was a gradual discovery, not a sudden invention, is proved by pottery found at Orvieto itself. There, in the immense amount of material excavated, we have in fact found fragments of vases with a green monochrome glaze on a smooth ground, or on a ground adorned with impressed reliefs. We have also found *panate* (pitchers with applied beaks) with designs traced in brown and green on the "biscuit," that is, on the bare body of the paste object; other pitchers in which the glaze has taken on noticeably yellow tints, perhaps from impurities in the lead; and jugs covered with white slip or with a rough white enamel which gradually improved in quality with the passage of time. The stages mentioned suggest the possibility of gradual discovery, and therefore of an evolution in which the knowledge of the late Middle Ages was linked with what we know of the initial development of majolica. The documents in the archives, which refer to one "Petrus vascellarius" in 1211, record the existence of a flourishing ceramic art, which is confirmed by the heraldic evidence offered by a plate with the armorial bearings of Charles d'Anjou, impaled with those of the Monaldeschi, and therefore executed before 1272, because from that year on the Angevins in Italy impaled with their own device the arms of Jerusalem.

Both these testimonies prove that the art of ceramics was flourishing in that center, encouraged by political and economic prosperity, at least from the thirteenth to the end of the fourteenth century. The documents in the archives, although understandably far from complete, throw some light on other localities also, mentioning a "Petrus orzolarius" in Faenza in 1142 and a "Martinus orciolarius" in Florence in 1195. Evidently there was much activity in ceramics in the twelfth century.

The ornamentation, when representational, drew its inspiration from a vegetable and animal repertory, sometimes with exotic subjects (as in the case of a camel painted on a Tuscan jug) or fantastic ones, but rarely human figures. The ornamentation was often geometric, epigraphic, heraldic, or religious. Whatever the theme, it adhered to the rigid Romanesque style, with clearly marked outlines, the background in trelliswork pattern with no attempt at creating a three-dimensional pictorial illusion or any expression of volume, and lacking any vibrant quality.

Suggestions from the East, whether Byzantine or Islamic, are evident, as is the influence of Moorish Spain and, still more, that of reconquered Spain. Equally strong is the evidence of local origins and the striking capacity for assimilation. The decorator transforms every element, however natural, into an abstract expression, a pure harmony of lines and colored surfaces, which remain only, as it were, skin deep and do not weaken the plasticity of the form.

The arrangement of the decorative design is not bound to any one scheme but generally tends to concentrate the observer's attention on one focal point. In hollow forms the distribution is often along horizontal bands or spread over the whole surface. In such examples the decoration is often contained within the zone on either side of the handle by vertical strips, by wedges, or by heads of birds in flight, painted in brown and surmounted by green braids or more rarely by dark-blue ones when the color scheme is dark blue and brown.

Below, the white ground of enamel or slip stops short of the base, which is generally made nonporous, like the backs of plates and dishes, with a simple coating of lead glaze. This method of confining the costly enamel to the surface destined to receive the decoration, which aims at economy in its use and speed and simplicity in execution, with the enamel-

ing and glazing done in two separate processes to avoid complications in the firing, was commonly used not only by Italian and Mediterranean potters but also by craftsmen in the Middle and Far East. This is evidence of similarities in work and of reciprocal influences through channels of communication which still elude identification.

The archaic type of vase reveals a unity of form and ornamentation that retained and ennobled its true values, without contaminating the purity of its expression by concessions of a pictorial or sculptural nature.

During the first half of the fifteenth century there appears, upon large dishes or *conche* from the Tuscan potteries, an ornamentation that was richer figuratively and more vibrant in form, indicating an increased awareness of the Gothic manner. The traditional brown-green palette (with the occasional addition of light yellow) with which these forms are expressed does not at once reveal innovations or revolutions in the technical field, apart from a greater daring shown in the production of exceptionally large vessels and an increased hardness in the vitreosity of the enamel, resulting from the considerable quantity of iron contained in the red clay from which these very large dishes had to be fashioned.

The more complex expression of this ornamentation led to the evolution of a style and technique that were to develop during the course of the century with a series of innovations in form and color that are certainly among the most successful in the long history of this art.

Gaetano Ballardini adopted for Italian majolica the chronology of Attic ceramics, whose stylistic evolution, to his mind, shows most affinity with that of Italy. The latter can therefore be more clearly described in terms applicable to Attic ceramics than in the usual sequence of Romanesque, Gothic, Renaissance, and Baroque. In fact, these customary classifications, applied also to architecture, painting, and sculpture, are not well chosen for

Stile severo

18

iii JAR WITH BOSS ORNAMENTATION AND DARK-GREEN GLAZE, FOUND IN ROMAN FORUM. PALEO-ITALIAN PERIOD (8TH OR 9TH CENT.). FAENZA MUSEUM. *iv* SICILIAN PLATES WITH FISH, BIRD, AND BRAID ORNAMENT. ARCHAIC PERIOD (14TH CENT.). GELA MUSEUM *v* LARGE ROUND DISH OF "FAMIGLIA VERDE" WITH HERALDIC LION AND BANNER OF FLORENCE. TUSCAN (FIRST HALF OF 15TH CENT.). PARIS, LOUVRE. *vi* DRUGPOT WITH SCROLLED LEAF AND "PEACOCK FEATHER" DECORATION. FAENZA (1470-80). LONDON, VICTORIA AND ALBERT MUSEUM.

vii

viii

ix

x

vii TWO-HANDLED DRUGPOT WITH "GOTHIC-FLORAL" DECORATION. FAENZA (1460–70). COPENHAGEN, DANSKE KUNSTINDUSTRIMUSEUM. *viii* PLATE WITH HERALDIC ARMS AND LEAVES, SGRAFFITO OVER SLIP. TUSCAN (16TH CENT.). THE HAGUE, GEMEENTEMUSEUM. *ix* MADONNA WITH CHILD AND ANGELS: LUNETTE FROM VIA DELL'AGNOLO (DETAIL). LUCA DELLA ROBBIA (CA. 1450). FLORENCE, BARGELLO. *x* MARBLE TOMB OF BISHOP BENOZZO FEDERIGHI. LUCA DELLA ROBBIA (1455). FLORENCE, CHURCH OF S. TRINITA.

the field of majolica. In his skillful study of the development of majolica Ballardini has therefore used for this period the term *stile severo* (severe style) to describe that sense of proportion and sobriety which still characterized the majolica artist and persisted for the whole of this period, that is, until the end of the fifteenth century. In this style the tendency is definitely in the direction of abstract, or nonnarrative, conceptions. The emphasis is on line and color, on composition, not on illustration, even when the geometric interlacing, the foliage, the radiating beams of light, the initials, the Sacred Monogram, or the heraldic emblems are replaced by human figures or animals which appear as types and not as individuals, and have value only as a linear or coloristic diversion, never as the theme or illustration of a story.

The wonderful achievements in color and ornament, stimulated by Gothic linearism and by Oriental models, and then, toward the end of the period, by monuments in the classical tradition, enabled Ballardini to classify the principal thematic motifs, which were superimposed, combined, and alternated.

The sense of the material is never lost, even though it is reduced by an enriched palette not long after the middle of the fifteenth century. The four fundamental colors, green, dark blue, orange-yellow, and purple, used on a covering glaze of brilliant white enamel were then spread, without economy, right down to the base of the hollow vases, and inside, as well as over the backs of plates and dishes. The vase and the plate both became increasingly varied in shape as they were adapted to growing uses in a life more complex and more active. Their shapes also became more elaborate as the potters, influenced by models in pewter, copper, and bronze, sought a greater freedom of line. Nevertheless, the shapes remained faithful to their practical function, and the ornamentation, however sumptuous, did not replace or diminish the formal values. With the cavity of the bowl framed by a wide or a narrow rim, it was transformed into a plate, but in both bowl and plate the sense of roundness still predominated and was emphasized by the scheme of decoration confined within concentric zones. Later examples, inspired by pewter—one with a deep well, a *tondino* or round dish, and one with a very shallow well, a *tagliere* or trencher—are more elaborate, according to the need which they supplied. The diameter is limited in proportion to the width of the rim, with the sense of the circular and spherical accentuated by the separation of the central motif, or ornamental rose, from the accompanying bands around the rim. When the decoration is not on circular bands, but on a flat plane, to use Piccolpasso's term, the ground is generally smooth, so as not to afford a contrast between the form and the ornamentation.

In the hollow ware, on the cylindrical sides of drugpots, and sometimes also on the rounded sides of globular or oval vases, the decoration is generally contained within superimposed parallel bands, which emphasize the sense of the horizontal and the circular movement. The bands are rarely vertical, never on vessels with convex sides, upon which they would strike a discordant note, lessening the impression of roundness.

On the jug which, because of the spout and handle, has a front and a back, the dominant element of decoration is usually concentrated within a frame that may be made of various things, such as a garland or a medallion, beneath the spout, and is accompanied by straps, tufted palms, horizontal rays, or by zones painted in *sopraccolore*, or by designs scattered over the ground in such a way as to harmonize with the shape of the jug. Sometimes, through the influence of this arrangement of decoration on the jug, drugpots and water jars as well, which do not offer a front and a back, have bands interrupted by medallions enclosing a single ornamental device. Also, the necessary indication of the contents on pharmacy jars creates a focal point in the illusion of a label with curled edges, with the inscription in Gothic characters or, more rarely, in Renaissance lettering. This may in itself constitute the only ornamental device on the white ground. Frequently, however, this label is inserted into the decorative scheme, which may include also the emblem of the pharmacy (which then becomes the central point of interest), or the decoration may be contained within circular bands.

Pavements In pavements, the excessive ornamentation on the individual tiles, which was the prevailing style until the end of the fifteenth century, could have led to confusion, but a harmonizing element is found in the common palette. Moreover, the difficulty in distinguishing the single decorative motif results in the pavement forming an over-all pattern of ornament in which, by contrast, the lines of the junctures of the tiles predominate and form, with geometric precision, the dominant motif.

Among the more common of these motifs are the regular diaper of squares, sometimes arranged in a checkerboard design with the squares painted in various colors; the honeycomb design, achieved by the use of tiles of regular polygonal shape; the more complicated design of crosses and squares, formed by the combination of elongated hexagons and squares; and the obviously Oriental design of crosses and stars. Another arrangement is of parallel intersecting toothed bands, obtained by using elongated hexagons alone, arranged side by side and all facing the same way. Sometimes the repetition of a strongly accentuated thematic motif or of a strikingly colored ground in tiles arranged in regular sequences may, over the whole surface of the pavement, produce a rhythmic scheme which sets off the decorative interplay afforded by the shapes and their distribution, as is usually to be seen in pavements formed of squares and elongated hexagons. In other examples, instead, the play of these forms is smothered by the geometric decorations themselves, which follow another pattern

and attract most attention. Here, however, the conception of each tile having its own self-sufficient design has been abandoned in favor of what is called the "over-all," or carpet, design, which was to be a distinguishing feature of later expressions.

These gradual discoveries of color and theme have, as we have said, enabled us to make some classifications. The first of these "families" appeared during the second quarter of the fifteenth century and is the *famiglia verde* (*famille verte*), which takes its name from the dominant color used and seems to belong more particularly to the Tuscan or, more precisely, the Florentine school. It presents no new technique: there is the green filling with brown outlines as in the preceding age, from which it differs only by its new conception of ornamentation. Famiglia verde; zaffera *group* / FIG. V

The family of *zaffera in rilievo* (cobalt blue in relief), the *Pastoseblau* of W. von Bode, or the "oak leaf" of Wallis, dating perhaps from a few years later, was produced during the same period in the potteries of Tuscany, in the Umbro-Latian region, and in the Romagna. When this style appears in Tuscany, which had given birth to the *famiglia verde*, the composition is generally more rich than elsewhere. The dominant motif is the leaf of the oak, or of the Turkey oak, which is distributed over the surface of two-handled globular jugs, sometimes framing a central theme, which is frequently an animal, a heraldic or a pharmaceutical device, or sometimes even a human figure. PL. 5

In the Romagna, at Faenza where the *famiglia verde* was almost unknown, the *zaffera in rilievo* style was closely related to the archaic phase, and therefore the compositions were usually simpler and more faithful to geometric schemes. The decorative themes here are usually armorial bearings, heraldic devices, initials enclosed within lobed and pointed cartouches, or within garlands with a double wreath of berries, painted upon the belly of the jug, and upon the plates, rosettes or animals framed in concentric wreaths of PL. 6

ivy or oak leaves. A rare tall-necked jug with a round body on a spreading foot, formerly in the collections of the International Museum of Ceramics in Faenza, but lost as a result of enemy action during the war, had, on a horizontal band running right around its body, the design of a trailing vine with rosettes and birds alternating, each bird with wings outspread and a berry in its beak.

The *zaffera in rilievo* family also derives its name from the dominant color, a thickly applied blackish blue, which replaces the green or is used at its side to give depth. The design was still always outlined in manganese brown. The name for cobalt blue, *zaffera*, spelled *zaffara* in fifteenth-century documents, is a popular adaptation of the Persian name, *al-safra*, given to the cobalt mineral from which the dark-blue color was extracted, which explains the origin of this contribution to Italian majolica. Byzantine findings during excavations at Constantinople and Islamic findings at Miletus have brought to light examples which reveal the kind of ornamentation in these regions. The Byzantine expressions were most akin to those of Italian ceramics.

Third in order of time came the family called "Italo-Moresque," to indicate that the inspiration and models, copied with considerable fidelity, were derived from the pottery of the Moors of Spain. The trade relations that Tuscany, more than any other Italian region, very busily maintained with Valencia and Catalonia and the work of agents of the merchants of Florence, Pisa, Lucca, and Prato, who kept banks and warehouses at Barcelona and Valencia, were both good means of acquainting the Italian cities with Spanish wares. Later on, vases and plates adorned with the austere but attractive iridescence of metallic luster, a peculiarity of the Spanish majolica, were imported in great quantity. As witness to the wide diffusion of this style there are vessels adorned with the heraldic arms of the Medici, Acciaioli, Arnolfi, Arrighi, Benvenuti, Dal Verre, Degli

Agli, Gentili, Gasconi, Morelli, Tedali, Zati, Mannucci, Spannocchi, and Tondi families. To these can be added some much rarer non-Tuscan examples, which belonged to the Sanchez of Naples, the Bonaccorsi of Ferrara, the House of Savoy, and the Orlyè of Turin, besides remains of pavements and pottery in Venice, Faenza, Bologna, and Naples, as well as Sicily and elsewhere.

To this continual flow of imports from Spain we owe the word "majolica." The name of the largest of the Balearic Islands, Majorca or Majolica, a port of call for ships in service between Spanish and Italian ports, was first introduced into Tuscany and then diffused through a large part of Italy. Even when these products were actually made in other places, such as Manises, near Valencia, or Barcelona, they were still brought to Tuscany in ships that came from Majorca, and so they were still called majolica products. They were vessels of clay covered with ivory-colored enamel and enriched with ornamentation in iridescent golden luster, to which a dark blue was sometimes added.

Toward the middle of the fifteenth century and later the popularity of this ware gave rise in Tuscany, and also in the Romagna, to local imitations in which the potters, not possessing the secret of the luster tones, used instead a threadlike manganese, or painted more extended surfaces in orange-yellow, to maintain a similarity with the color schemes of the much-prized models.

Dark blue, green, yellow, and manganese brown, which when used diluted in large patches takes on a purple tone, were the colors of this group, which was the first to show the full fifteenth-century palette, whose luminous tonality, however, was yet to be fully revealed. The fondness for Spanish luster naturally prepared the way also for the more or less faithful imitation of monochrome decoration in dark blue.

It is difficult to trace the transition from the Italo-Moresque family to that called the "Gothic-floral family" because of the prevalence in both of flower and leaf designs, and the fondness of both for Gothic styles and models, either inspired by architectural elements or the fantasy of the miniature illuminators. Also, the Oriental influence persists, coming from the Middle East as well as from Spain itself.

In Faenza this transition is manifested in a style that has been identified as the "cold palette" school, characterized by a hard and brilliant coating of enamel, generally of considerable thickness, upon which a blackish gray-blue, a pale lime yellow, a green, and a purple are used for flower and leaf as well as for figurative ornamentation in which the Moorish features are gradually superseded by the predominating Gothic elements. Tuscany, and perhaps Umbria, used the same colors to paint Moorish as well as Gothic patterns, but its ceramists did not have the advantage of a fine and brilliant enamel like that used in the workshops of the Adriatic centers, which from this time on were developing a variety of composition scarcely ever surpassed.

The palette now acquired warmth through the substitution of orange for lime yellow; the purple, like the dark blue, became more pellucid, and the green was lit by yellow *sfumature*. All this, in the second half of the fifteenth century, accompanied the appearance of the Gothic-floral family, which was on the whole the richest in fantasy and the most effective in the use of color.

The flora offered a wide field, which was largely drawn upon by decorators who stylized their models so much as to render them almost unrecognizable. A long scrolled FIG. *vi* leaf often springs from a tufted branch upon which hangs the fruit in the form of an elongated bulb swollen at one end, which might perhaps recall the "onions" of architectural spires and pinnacles were it not for the smooth form and the love of the fantastic which are more reminiscent of the style of the illuminators. In Tuscany, in Northern Italy, and in the South, the leaf tends to straighten out, but in Faenza and the rest of

the Romagna it keeps its vigorous curves. A four-petaled rosette, or a twig with three bulbous flowers, occupies the center of the dish or the oval medallion of the jugs, when these are not adorned with heraldic or epigraphic motifs, or human and animal figures, the latter being enclosed within a "contour panel" which follows more or less closely FIG. *vii* the outline of the figure. This contour panel, softened by slight shading of the inner edge toward the middle, recalls a treatment frequently observed in Middle Eastern pottery. St. Bernardino's device of the Sacred Initials PL. 9b surrounded by rays of light, with its powerfully evocative emotional appeal, constituted one of the most important motifs in the ornamental scheme. Around the rim of the dish were varied designs of festoons and arcading, fan palms, knolls indicated with a few robust slanting strokes, chains with straight or curved links, crossed poles, and so on, often connected with the central motif by bands of green and orange, or sometimes of green, orange, and dark blue, cleverly set off by the white ground—in all of which arrangements the artist shows a thorough understanding of the principle of complementary colors.

The inspiration from nature does not prevent the evolution, by means of the process of stylization, of geometric forms, which nonetheless preserve in their patterns the memory of the original form. For example, we find some rosettes in which the petals have been replaced by a few radiating brush strokes placed at the top of the straight stalks arranged crosswise. Sometimes the starting point of the design is a spray with its three flowers merely suggested by slanting brush strokes.

It would be impossible to complete an analysis of the motifs used in decoration—so great is the wealth of fancy and the variety of interpretation. As we have said, the Gothic-floral family constitutes the most important nucleus during the period of the *stile severo*, and it is certainly the richest

22

determinant of the character of the whole age.

Peacock feather group

PL. 9a

PL. 8

PL. 10

One element that was already tentatively revealed in Gothic-floral ornamentation, in which it seems to have originated, was to assert itself independently later on, in the last thirty years of the fifteenth century. This was the "peacock's feather eye," the *Pfauaugenmuster* as Bode called it, the "peacock" as it is still briefly described today in the workshops of the Faenza potters. The motif is of distant Oriental origin, as is proved by its appearance on painted vases of the early metal age found at Tepe Mussian during the excavations conducted by De Morgan at the beginning of the century. Almost certainly, in this primitive expression, the motif alluded to the rising sun and appeared, in the beginning still undefined, in borders of polychrome arcading of varying width with minute radiating lines, painted around the rim of plates of the floral family, and later on as an accompaniment to the motif of the scrolled leaf. In its mature form it is used as the motif for a border on plates or vases, either in the shape of a feather, or set in a semicircle, or as a dominant motif, arranged in an overlapping design or within a wide diaper pattern, so as to cover broad surfaces of vases. The beauty of the ornament, painted in an ocherous yellow, which is in fact called "peacock yellow," accompanied by dark blue and green, with the occasional addition of purple, lies in the minute rhythmic distribution of the fundamental tints. Here we have the full supremacy of color asserted over form and line. In this motif of the peacock feather the potter displays with superlative skill the brilliance of the vitreous enamel.

Persian palmette group; the pavement of S. Petronio in Bologna

PL. 11

Contemporary with the peacock's feather is the family of the Persian palmette and rosette, which Bode defines as the *Granadapfelmuster*, or pomegranate, motif. As interpreted in the simplest way by the Italian potters, it takes the form of a round fruit, rather like a pine cone when seen in vertical or in horizontal section. It has many variants, including one which resembles the flower of the thistle. It is obviously of Middle Eastern origin; its prototypes are found, painted in luster or in polychrome, on Persian tiles and vases from Kashan, Rhages, Gurgan, and Veramin of the beginning of the thirteenth century and on later Syrian, Egyptian, and Turkish pottery. It is not confined to ceramic ware but is frequently found on other materials, particularly textiles and carpets.

The Persian palmette motif was very widely used in the workshops of Faenza and its sphere of influence, and by the potters of Tuscany and Umbria. One may distinguish between the two groups by noting the more noticeable rotundity of the Faventine designs as compared with a certain flattening in those of Tuscany. Moreover, Faenza, with the advantage of its more intensely vitreous enamel, showed a more careful and more sophisticated sense of color in the filling of the ground of the lobed borders.

PL. 12

The fullest use made of the Persian palmette motif known to us today is seen in the vertical tiles of the altar steps and in the borders of the majolica pavement of the Chapel of S. Sebastiano in the Church of S. Petronio in Bologna. Completed by the majolica workers of Faenza in 1487 under the direction and at the expense of the parish priest Donato Vaselli, this pavement consists of regular hexagonal tiles with a separate design on each tile, set in borders and frames of rectangular tiles which all bear the constant alternating motifs of the rosette and palm. There are 1,083 tiles, and the pavement gives us the richest and most complete example of the fantastic repertory of ornament at the disposal of a majolica workshop of that period.

The artist Pietro Andrea, who portrayed himself in the act of painting, seated outside his workshop, has used the familiar ornamental motifs of majolica potters, including those of the floral family, the peacock feather, and the Persian palmette, with heraldic devices and cartouches bearing mottoes of popular wisdom and names of artists, with figures of animals and male and female human busts, with instruments and tools, all contained within ornamental borders. He has also introduced elements derived from the ornaments of classical architecture and from the fantasy of decorators, painters, or engravers of Renaissance inspiration. Thus we frequently find among the tiles in S. Petronio bisons, pearls and eggs, braids, festoons, skulls of oxen, polychrome grotesques, all those features, in fact, which prove that during the last twenty years of that century —for we must assume that the vast application on this pavement was preceded by some practice, however limited, in the workshop— the spirit of the Renaissance had penetrated the potters' studios, although it did not yet express itself on a narrative plane. Indeed, in the course of a few years, it was to completely transform the decorator's way of thinking and consequently his repertory of ornament.

It is somewhat surprising not to find in the pavement tiles of S. Petronio any sign of the decoration called *alla porcellana*, a decoration which drew its inspiration—indirectly, through examples made in the Near East (in old documents it was in fact called Damascene decoration)—from the rare and exotic Chinese porcelain of the Ming dynasty. Perhaps the monochrome dark-blue ornamentation, faithful to its original, did not attract Pietro Andrea and his collaborators, who made great use of color in their pavement; possibly the motif, which was to be one of the most widely diffused and most productive of fantasy and variations during the first half of the following century, had not been introduced into Pietro's workshop. But this is hard to believe, for recent discoveries in Faenza have confirmed the fact that the appearance of the "porcelain" decoration was contemporary with the ornamentation of the Gothic-floral and Persian palmette families, as well as with the first tentative appearances of Renaissance grotesques painted in thread-

like white upon more or less intense blue and lavender-gray (*berettino*) enamel.

There has been an attempt to identify in the chapel pavement tiles the hand of the painter responsible for other ornamentation in the church—of Costa, for example, the author of the altarpiece, or of some other Bolognese to whom its markedly Renaissance character could be attributed. Unfortunately, there is not sufficient documentation of the relations and the negotiations between the patron and the artists, and so the attempt remains unsuccessful. In any case we cannot exclude the contribution of the majolica tradition, which is evident in innumerable details.

The taste for strong and clearly drawn ornamental forms was realized on the one hand by polychrome painted decoration on enamel and on the other hand by incising the coating of clay slip to expose the reddish color of the body.

The slip, mentioned in the archaic period as a preliminary step in the introduction of enamel, was never abandoned in the potters' workshops, not even when enamel was in general use. If in some of these workshops enamel became the usual, or even the only, ground for decoration, in others, and not always merely for reasons of economy, the ground remained the clay slip. It was generally the particular style favored by the individual potter that determined which coating was used, but in some places we see not so much a definite choice as a separation of styles, both of which may easily have been developed at the same time within the same workshop.

Among such centers must be mentioned Faenza, famous for its dishes, bowls, and vases of the archaic period, with their delicate designs traced with a fine point upon a pale straw-colored clay in a style which hardly needed the white clay slip under the colorless glaze, marbled with green and brown specks and patches. In the "severe"

Faïence covered with slip and sgraffito under glaze

24

period the lines were more decidedly and strongly incised, and there were sometimes characteristic figures or types. The incisions now exposed a brick-red clay and were accompanied by patches and crosshatching in brown, green, and, more rarely, dark blue. One must admit, however, that in the pottery centers, such as Faenza, the color distracted from the concentration on the incised line which is most effectively used in localities not dominated by enamel work. Among these may be numbered the Emilian centers of

PLS. 13 a, b

Ferrara and Bologna, in which the highly developed architectonic use of undressed brick and ornamental terracotta constitutes a permanent memorial to ceramic art. The Venetian centers of Padua and Venice, Lombardy, and some places in Tuscany must be included also. In all these localities pottery

PL. 14

with a clay slip and sgraffito decoration became predominant, and the designs were full of vitality. In the colored decoration irregular patches of green and tawny brown, very common in Emilia, are matched by green, brown, and dark gray-blue in the Venetian centers, which used these colors also for filling in. Lombardy is more susceptible to the Emilian fashion. The Tuscan potters do not usually interpose any coloring oxide between the slip and the glaze, and the decoration therefore depends upon incisions which expose the yellowish body, making a

FIG. viii

delicate contrast with the ivory of the slip. In these workshops, and in many others, the glazes used are all monochrome, green, tawny yellow, or, more rarely, dark blue or purple. Sometimes the marbled surfaces are left without sgraffito decoration.

The designs that, generically considered, might seem the same as those used in enameled ware, can, when closely examined, be clearly differentiated. A typical motif is the trailing vine or the ground decorated with scrolled leaves with very deeply indented edges, or the leafy spray, or large mulberries, or leaves with edges that curl back and in, thus accentuating the pointed outline. The

hedges of the "gardens of love," inspired by contemporary woodcuts, have skies streaked with lines of tiny dots.

Then came the clay modelers who enriched the potter's vases, drugpots, and bowls with rope moldings, fringes, and other embellishments. They molded handles, bases, and other complementary parts in the form of figures, thus distracting the eye from the simple geometric outline of the form. Frequently the artist gave free rein to his imagination in creating objects that had no connection with pottery vessels. He modeled religious or secular images in low relief or in the round, sometimes even groups of figures which the potter then completed with enamel and polychrome decoration, thus distinguishing the ceramic product from sculpture. In fact, even if the *raison d'être* of pottery lay in its fulfilling a useful function, this cardinal principle was slowly allying itself with another: that of delighting the eye. The danger of excessive realism in polychrome, a danger which is present to a still greater degree in terracottas and in wooden figures decorated with stucco and polychrome, is avoided by the ingenuous stylization of the forms, still bound to the Gothic pattern—jagged clefts in the earth, straight square rocks, robes with ornamental folds, and the absence of color in the fleshy parts, such as the hands and faces, in which only the features of eyes, mouth, and nose are emphasized with abrupt conventional strokes on the white enamel.

Mention of the small plastic works by potters leads inevitably to a discussion of the work of the Della Robbias, of Luca and his contemporaries, his nephews, and his later followers. Their works belong legitimately to the field of ceramics because of the material used and the combination of plasticity and color. Even when sculptors have expressed their fantasies in glazed terracotta rather than in marble or bronze, these works belong, because of their origins, to a world different

Ceramic sculpture

PLS. 15, 16, 17, 18, 19

PL. 17

Luca della Robbia and his successors

FIG. ix

from the traditional field of ceramics, inspired as most are, especially in the early period of Luca and his contemporaries, by a powerful mystical conception, which becomes most dramatic with Andrea and which is expressed in a volumetric vocabulary.

Glazing has made clay everlasting, as Vasari rightly points out, but it has not diminished or influenced its plastic values, which remain supreme. It is also true that Luca —and Brunelleschi and Ghiberti in their more limited attempts—does not seem to have absorbed anything from the potter's art except the method of work and some complementary architectural elements and applications. Conversely, during and after a whole century of their work, and in spite of the undeniable tendency toward coloristic expression already obvious in Andrea but still more pronounced in Giovanni, his brothers, followers, and imitators, contemporary potters and those of a later age do not seem to have absorbed anything from the whole Della Robbian œuvre.

A useful parallel to the relation between the Della Robbia plastics and the work of the potters may be found by comparing Etruscan statues with Etruscan vases, whether painted or adorned with reliefs. Of course, it is not possible to measure them by the same standards or to consider the vases as creations comparable in artistic sensibility to the great statues that in archaic and Hellenistic times decorated temple pediments—such as the Apollo of Veii and the Apollo from Falerium at Villa Giulia.

The Della Robbia movement, which must be included among expressions of ceramic art, remained alien to the central tradition of the majolica workshops. It was a separate phenomenon and neither a product of the workshops nor an adaptation.

Having made this clear, we must also point out that the Della Robbia achievement cannot be used as an excuse for setting up a scale of values, in the sense of a major plastic art with a minor expression in the potter's craft. The artistic phenomenon expresses itself in infinitely varied ways. The potter's art, complex as it is, takes into consideration and turns to its use volumetric and coloristic qualities, together with the brilliance of vitreous material, and moves upon a plane of its own, making one harmonious whole of plastic and pictorial material. The sculptor's art, which considers plastic values and effects of light and shadow, moves upon another plane. Both aim at expressing, by different means, a world that responds to the senses and to the imagination, and it is only upon the basis of power of expression and successful realization that hierarchical classifications may be attempted.

Luca della Robbia, who confined full and free coloristic expression to his wreaths of fruit and flowers, was evidently susceptible, above all, to those elements with which the sculptor expresses himself: mass and light. His spiritual Madonnas are in white enamel, of a softened brilliance, and the background, from which they stand out in relief, is usually all in blue monochrome. The brown markings of the eyebrows and eyes do not interrupt the harmony of the masses and the flowing lines. In fact, Luca is above all a worker in marble and derives his artistic expression from the purity of that material, as may be seen in the Cantoria of the Opera del Duomo in Florence and in the tomb of Bishop Benozzo Federighi in S. Trinita, also FIG. X in Florence, as well as in the tabernacle of Peretola.

On the other hand, Luca reveals himself as a most ardent colorist and ceramist, with a full understanding of the just measure of each contributory element—color, form, and brilliance—in his ornamental detail. He rarely paints the whole of a work in color, but when he does so it is because he cannot or will not display his plastic powers. The roundels with the emblems of the Guilds in Orsanmichele and the panel with the arms of René d'Anjou at the Victoria and Albert Museum in London are cases in point. In the lunette with the Eternal Father, in the Museum of the Opera

xi

xii

xiii

xi PLATE AND DRUGPOT WITH BLUE "PORCELAIN" DECORATION. FAENZA (LATE 15TH CENT.). FAENZA MUSEUM. *xii* DISH WITH "PORCELAIN" DEC-
ORATION: HEART AND OTHER MOTIFS. FAENZA (LATE 15TH CENT.). MILAN, GIOVANNI BOLOGNESI COLL. *xiii* PLATE WITH "PORCELAIN" DECORATION.
CAFAGGIOLO (FIRST HALF OF 16TH CENT.). BOLGHERI, COUNT UGOLINO DELLA GHERARDESCA COLL.

common to other majolica workshops. The Della Robbian colors, as is well known, are hardly ever as flowing, and their vocabulary of design generally consists of geometric patterns or imitations of Oriental drapery with even the fringes sometimes copied.

These details had already been used by Luca in the friezes of the gable and base of the marble altar of Peretola (1442) in which we see the beginning of the use of majolica. Later on, in Peretola and in Florence in the Portuguese Cardinal's Chapel in S. Miniato, in S. Trinita in the Chapel of the Crucifix (formerly at S. Miniato), at the Impruneta, and in the Pazzi Chapel in S. Croce, this plastic ornamentation was extended and developed by Luca's heirs and imitators. Andrea's work is seen in the Chapel of the Stigmata at La Verna, in the prison chapel at Prato, in the Cathedral porch at Pistoia, in the Fraternità di S. Maria del Latte at Montevarchi, at the Collegiata of Empoli and the Church of S. Giacomo Maggiore at Bologna. To Giovanni are attributed various dark-blue glazed vases, some of them with flowers, all adorned with arabesques and gadroons, in the niche of S. Pietro Martire in S. Domenico at Arezzo; to Luca the Younger the many Roman pavements at the Vatican and at S. Silvestro al Quirinale, and in Florence at the Palazzo Vecchio.

Form and color fully developed; Far Eastern influence; "porcelain" styles

As was proved by the designs of the tiles in S. Petronio, the spirit of the Renaissance did not suddenly manifest itself in the majolica workshops, but gradually emerged in forms, images, and conceptions based on the new vision. Developments in color now offered possibilities of a more complex decorative expression. The world of the imagination, opened to cultured patrons by the more humanistic way of thinking and the more intimate knowledge of the history and myths of ancient times, was a powerful source of inspiration. The serene architectonic harmonies of the Tuscan palaces, now universally known and admired, as well as their shapes and ornamentation, exercised a moderating influence. The art of printing, facilitating the diffusion of pictures, led to more complex representations, so that, toward the end of the fifteenth century and at the beginning of the sixteenth, the purely linear and coloristic conception became allied to the desire for narrative representation, which found its exponents in the masters of what has been aptly described as the first *istoriato*, or pictorial narrative, style.

From the moment the Gothic-floral style first appeared, the decorators had frequently indulged in more or less complex designs, generally inspired by amatory episodes or symbols, or by Christian piety, within a border of abstract ornamentation.

These representations, limited, tentative, and rough at first, began then to improve. At the same time, they were surrounded by interlacing knotted bands in *sopraccolore*, shapes continuous or subdivided into radiating compartments like metopes and triglyphs on the rim of the plate, with broken bastions, woven braids, or other designs as substitutes for complementary thematic motifs, which, together with the Persian palmette, generally accompanied the grotesques. The shading became softer, the enamel (in some potteries) more vitreous, and the sides of dishes and pots thinner in imitation of the fine, exotic porcelain. All this struck a new note and gave a new trend to the potters' art.

The shape of the plate is now enlivened by the wavy lines of the well and rim, without hard angles, and probably reflects delicate elegant Sung shapes. The heavy bowls, with wide wells resting on foot rings, and narrow horizontal rims, give place to more delicate plates or bowls with flat surfaces lightly indented for greater steadiness, and with a scalloped edge. The semicircular bowls are replaced by bell-shaped ones, with a slightly protruding lip. The *tondini* appear, bowls with deep wells and wide rims, as do the *taglieri*, or large trenchers, with very shallow wells, both forms wrought in imitation of pewter models. Besides the potbellied footless jug, the small flask with a foot and a long neck appears. In the pharmacies the drugpots have straight smooth sides, with rope moldings above and below; sometimes they show a slight swelling toward the top, like an overturned cone, and are occasionally without lids; the spherical flasks with long necks take the place of the two-handled jars. We frequently find the small jug with a long curving tubular spout sometimes molded to look like the neck of a dragon or some other beast. The purity and the functional character of the shape are respected even when the pictorial ornamentation begins to assert its supremacy.

Certainly the potters were by no means unaffected by their knowledge of that exotic product, porcelain, so different in structure and character from Western pottery. Porcelain was at first imported into Europe in more or less limited quantities, brought by the trading ships of the seafaring republics of Venice and Genoa and along the routes of Persia and Egypt; later on, after the circumnavigation of Africa by Portuguese and Dutch navigators, it was much more widely diffused.

Marco Polo was the first, in his *Milione*, to give it the name *porcellana* because of its resemblance to a compact white shell of that name, commonly found in the inlets of the Persian Gulf and the Red Sea. Ever since his day, porcelain has been prized and coveted by the rich and powerful. We know that the rare examples were jealously preserved, and listed as precious objects in inventories. Even miraculous qualities were sometimes attributed to them.

In Europe, at the end of the fifteenth century, Italian potters attempted to make porcelain. In 1470, M. Antonio, the alchemist, tried in Venice; in 1518, also in Venice, Leonardo Peringer; later on, in Ferrara through the initiative of Duke Alfonso II, and in Turin, through that of Duke Emanuele Filiberto, other attempts were made, as also at Pesaro, encouraged by Duke Guidobaldo II,

and finally, in Florence in 1575, the only place where the attempt met with some success. There, under the patronage and with the personal encouragement of Prince, later Grand Duke, Francis I, porcelain continued to be made until the year 1587.

However, attempts were made to copy the technical process, which, continued under the patronage of Francis's heirs, Ferdinando and Cosimo II in Florence, and renewed by Manfredo Settala in Milan in the seventeenth century, led to manufacture of the French "soft paste" porcelain. These attempts, however, did not have the same success as those which aimed merely at copying the external aspects (form, color, decoration) and adopted the common ceramic materials—in the Middle East, a siliceous compound and in the West, colored clay and white enamel.

The busy trade between the Middle East and the Far East, which supplied the Chinese with the cobalt mineral from which they extracted the dark-blue color, had widely diffused porcelain in the Middle Eastern lands. On these porcelains, under the Yuan dynasty (1271-1367) and still more under the Ming (1368-1644), the blue and white decoration had become predominant. The Chinese took many features, together with the fondness for dark blue, from the Middle East, but many more elements seem to have originated in the Far East, so that Persia and, later on, Mesopotamia, Syria, and Egypt became intermediaries for the diffusion of the designs that embellished the much-prized Ming porcelains in the lands of the Mediterranean basin and thence throughout the whole of Europe.

The terms "damascene color," "decorated *alla damaschina*," which are found in documents of the late fifteenth and the beginning of the sixteenth century, together with, or instead of, the indication *a porcellana* or *alla porcellana* to designate the blue color and the decorations in the Syriac-Persian style, are evidence of the route followed by those wares on their way to the Italian shops. At the end of the fifteenth century and for a large part of the sixteenth, these shops showed a particular taste for those exotic designs, a taste manifested in the assimilation of forms and of decorative schemes.

The Italian potters' vigorous power of assimilation was at first overcome in wonder aroused by these new elements which they copied so closely. They imitated the border designs as well as the central figures—silkworm, reed, bird, duck, drum, disk, rosette, and twig—which were set against intensely stylized landscapes and skies, sometimes with the addition of trophies, masks, hearts, or busts. The borders are ornamented with a continuous trailing spray sometimes interrupted by a flower with lobed petals that looks rather like a lotus or chrysanthemum. The spray is adorned with minute leaves and the tiny flower that botanists in fact call the "porcelain flower" (Guasti actually refers to the potters' use of this name for the motif rather than to the name as used for the ware itself). This flower sometimes hangs in bands like lively little festoons, with the tiny leaves drawn in rapid brush strokes. Later on, with the widespread diffusion of this ware, began the slow process of assimilation, which, toward the end of the sixteenth century, led to the disintegration of the elements of composition, which were then rearranged in geometric schemes and thus lost their original character, grown stale by long use. The monotony of the dark blue was broken, in these later products, by the addition of orange and yellow.

The use of other colors with the dark blue is rare in examples of the fifteenth century and during the first half of the sixteenth century. When it occurs it is a sign of the adulteration of the "porcelain" motif with others of Western origin, such as we find, for example, in a "porcelain" border around a central design of a figure, trophy, or mask, and, vice versa, a wreathed or festooned border for a "porcelain" center.

The love of the exotic was more evident in the products of the workshops of the Faventine group, the first to get possession of the models (which came perhaps through Venice) toward the end of the fifteenth century, than in those at Cafaggiolo. There, in the villa on the slopes of the Tuscan-Emilian Apennines, Pierfrancesco, a member of a younger branch of the Medici, directed the workshop during the last years of the fifteenth century and, more successfully, during the first decade of the sixteenth century. Pierfrancesco had the help of potters from Montelupo and artists from Florence, and kept an attentive eye on the workshops of Faenza. Exoticism was no longer seen in the work, obviously influenced by the new "porcelain" style, produced at Montelupo, which, if only for the volume of ware produced, ranks as one of the greatest centers of Tuscan ceramic production.

In Siena, Master Benedetto introduced from Faenza designs that were already westernized. At Deruta, in the neighborhood of Perugia, the "porcelain" motif does not seem to appear at all. At most, this center, as we shall see, welcomed a form of decoration better described as arabesque, although distorted and by then somewhat outworn. In Latium, and more precisely in Rome, the presence of potters from all over led to the appearance of the "porcelain" motif among others, but here also it was divested of its original character.

The popularity of exoticism had refined both form and taste, had introduced a new and vigorous growth of thematic motifs and, more important still, a fondness for monochrome decoration. It can and must be considered as an expression of the longing for novelty, fed by the spirit of the Renaissance, and with it the period of the *stile severo* draws to its end.

In the period of transition from linear and incisively colored motifs to a narrative style in which expressions of religious piety and of a newborn interest in Humanistic knowledge and culture (products of the Neoplatonic philosophy so widely diffused among the pa-

FIG. xi

FIG. xii

FIG. xiii

The Humanistic approach

30

xviii PLATE WITH DEATH OF VIRGIN. FAENZA, MASTER OF THE DEATH OF THE VIRGIN (CA. 1510). LONDON, BRITISH MUSEUM.

31

trons of art) were mingled or alternated, the work of the masters of the early *istoriato*, or pictorial narrative, style made its appearance, accompanied, as is to be expected, by a rich repertory of abstract motifs.

PL. 32 The period is well characterized by a group of intensely polychromed pharmacy vases which have been variously attributed to the workshops of Faenza, Deruta, and Siena. By general agreement these vases are now assigned to the series to which the Colonna-Orsini vase belongs, because of the emblematic representation of the Pax Romana of 1511, seen on a comparatively late flask in the British Museum. These diverse attributions, each one well supported by arguments worthy of consideration, are the proof of a fact not often willingly admitted; that is, because of the mobility of the products and the emigration of the artisans it is not always possible to distinguish with certainty between the typical wares of the various workshops, and therefore it is advisable to proceed with the greatest caution in assigning places of origin.

In this specific case the characteristics of color and enamel, and some details of ornament, such as the dark-blue lozenge cut crosswise, would seem to indicate the workshops of Faenza, while a certain rigidity in the drawing of the figures and some elements in the flower and plant decoration of the sections are reminiscent of the designs of the Deruta workshops, which, in their turn, were attributed to those of Siena.

Masters of the early istoriato at Faenza With these masters the first personalities emerge from the anonymous mass. Identification is still tentative, and rarely attested by a name or a mark, but already presents characteristic features that make possible some classification and differentiation. It is one of the peak periods of the art of Faenza.

The master whom Rackham calls the "Painter of St. John" (with affinities to the so-called "Caricature Painter") is considered to be the author of the St. John, after an engraving by Marcantonio, at the Victoria and Albert Museum. This work is related to a series of other dishes and plates showing figures with noticeably distorted features, such as the Eritrean Sibyl formerly in the Frassineto Collection in Florence, of which the Painter of St. John is generally assumed to be the author. Others in this group are attributed to the Caricature Painter, including a Baker at Work, formerly in the collection of the Marquis d'Azeglio and reproduced in Delange's *Recueil* of 1869, and the Doge Barbarigo PL. 28 watching the Loading of the Moneybags, in the Fitzwilliam Museum of Cambridge (Leverton Harris Coll.). To these may be added a series of female busts, painted over the whole surface of the plate, like the superb "Giulia Bella" at the Faenza Museum, and some less PL. 29 important "lovers' dishes," always with busts PLS. 30, 31 of "Fair Ladies," generally framed by rims adorned with pomegranates or with borders in polychrome and *sopraccolore*.

The Master C. I. or G. I. (the lettering is PL. 33 not clear) who places his initials both on the front and on the back of a plate, in the Hermitage of Leningrad (Basilewsky Coll.), with figures painted in blue and orange on a yellow ground, is, according to Rackham, the author of a remarkable group of other works painted in polychrome with a light and graceful effect in form and line.

In a different group from that of the Master C. I. are two series of works which greatly resemble each other. One of these may be attributed to the Master of the Death of the Virgin, or Master Gonela, from the plate in FIG. xviii the British Museum, with the composition from an engraving by Martin Schongauer, painted with sharply pleated folds in tones of dark blue and amethyst, and from the inscriptions on the back of a bowl formerly in the Damiron Collection in Lyons, painted with figures of prisoners. The other group is that of the Monogrammist P. F., or "painter from the workshop of Francesco Torelli," who, in 1522, painted in dark blue with faint yellow shading the center of a plate with the Doubting Thomas, now in a private English collection. To the former group Ballardini and Rackham ascribe also a small plate with Dürer's Christ before Annas and a basin with the Judgment of Solomon, at the Victoria and Albert Museum, as well as a plate with Dürer's Christ before Pilate at the Museo Civico of Bologna. To the second group should be assigned a panel with Christ washing St. Peter's Feet, at the Victoria and Albert Museum. In this series should also probably be included the large plate with trophies and the Farnese coat of arms, with the signature of Piero del Castello, in the Museo Civico of Bologna, and some tiles that were originally in S. Biagio at Forlì, later transported to Pieve di Quinto, and now preserved in the Victoria and Albert Museum.

The Painter of the Assumption is so called from the painting on a panel at the Victoria and Albert Museum which resembles the tile at the British Museum with the Sacrifice of Isaac, after a Titianesque engraving. To him also are ascribed some small plates with the mark of Casa Pirota, one of which, formerly in the Beit Collection in London, has a scene with grotesques, dated 1520. The known *œuvre* of this painter might be increased by the addition of plates recently unearthed in excavations near Faenza, very closely related to the types which Master Benedetto was to introduce into Siena about this time.

The Lucretia Painter derives his title from the plate in the Museo Civico of Bologna showing the Death of Lucretia. The Master of Selene is the name given to the painter of the basin at the Bargello in Florence, which has a large central scene painted in dark blue and compound colors, framed by a rim in intense polychrome.

PL. 35

The Master of the Resurrection derives his name from a tile at the Victoria and Albert Museum in which the painter recalls a composition by Dürer, with a delicate tonal play of azures, pale yellows and ambers, greens and amethysts, and which, because of the monogram BT (or TB) on the back of another panel with the same characteristics, at the Bargello, representing the Martyrdom of

PL. 36

St. Sebastian, has also been ascribed to the Monogrammist B. T. This mark, which may indicate the workshop rather than the name of the painter, is found also on certain plates —one flat dish, decorated all over with trophies, at the Victoria and Albert Museum, and another with a well, decorated with musical emblems, a woman and some naked children set in a landscape, now in the British Museum, as well as on a drugpot with the bust of a man, also at the British Museum. There is also the indication of the workshop of a Master Ieronimo da Forlì whose name is written in full on the back of another plate, in the Victoria and Albert Museum, with the scene of Christ among the Doctors enclosed in a bizarre border of weapons, implements, and musical instruments of every kind, painted in blue monochrome. This indication, together with the monogram BT, authorizes us to conclude that the Master of the Resurrection was a wandering artist, that is, not tied to a single workshop but working freely, in Faenza, now at one shop and now at another. To him Rackham also attributes the plate with David and Goliath, at the Bargello in Florence, dated 1507, a bowl with Dürer's Deposition of Christ, within a frame of grotesques and busts with shields, dated 1519, and a panel with the same subject, of Mantegnesque inspiration, dated 1523, both at the Victoria and Albert Museum. His manner is also seen in the larger panel with the representation of the Fall of Man, after Marcantonio's engraving of Raphael's picture, also dated 1523. If we accept Falke's attribution of the bowl formerly in the Damiron Collection at Lyons, with Nymphs Bathing, dated 1503, we may confine the work of the Resurrection Master roughly to the first quarter of the century.

PL. 37

The dispersal of masters as well as products from the workshops of Faenza rapidly popularized the typical forms of their art. We find Master Benedetto di Giorgio da Faenza in Siena, where he had been residing since 1503. He had set up an important workshop in the

Siena potteries

33

quarter of the Porta S. Marco and was a member of the Confraternita di S. Lucia, in which he rose to the position of Consul. Between 1518 and 1520 he produced a considerable quantity of pottery for the Ospedale di S. Maria della Scala. In 1541 he married off a daughter to another Faventine potter, resident in Siena. Master Benedetto signed a plate, now in the Victoria and Albert Museum, which has in the center the image of St. Jerome in the Desert, painted in dark blue with touches of white pigment for the highlights, with a border of interlacing ribbons, linked by arabesque motifs to the narrow band of tiny leaves, related to "porcelain" flowers, which run around the outer edge of the rim. Other polychrome pieces, with or without the marks B°, M°, B, I.P., decorated with grotesques on a pale-yellow or amber ground or, less often, on a dark-blue ground, and sometimes accompanied by scenes with figures, reveal a relationship with the Faventine models. Some of them show a marked resemblance to the work of the masters of the early *istoriato* style, for example, to that of the above-mentioned Painter of the Assumption.

FIGS. *xiv, xv*

The Sienese masters also produced some remarkable pavements. Less elaboration of design is shown in that which adorns the Piccolomini library of the Cathedral. The library walls were decorated by Pinturicchio and completed by him in 1507, the year in which we may assume the pavement was set in place. Every tile shows the heraldic device of the Crescent within a braided border painted in polychrome. More complicated, both in structure and in decoration, with highly fantastic polychrome grotesques and the Piccolomini and Petrucci arms, was the pavement dated 1509, which was formerly in the Palazzo del Magnifico, also in Siena, and is now dispersed in various museums outside the country.

The Sienese workshops showed a characteristic fondness for rather small grotesques, and a dark blackish color which was frequently used for filling in the grounds.

It is not far from Siena to Deruta, in the neighborhood of Perugia. The strongly marked characteristics of the Deruta types do not reveal such close contacts with the Faventine masters as do those of Siena, except in the case of those potters who decorated the backs of dishes with the familiar daisy petals, common to the Faventine workshops, but found also at Siena and Cafaggiolo. At Deruta, as at Siena, this motif is accompanied by initials, singly or in groups.

The use of a coating of white slip beneath the enamel, with the back of the dish only glazed—as is common on the sturdy plates or trenchers of large dimensions—the conventional design, the faithful adherence to "severe" styles, the typical division of the decoration on the rim into alternating sections in the manner of metopes and triglyphs, the center decorated with characteristic busts, heraldic arms, or, more rarely, complicated scenes illustrating popular proverbs—all are unmistakable features of the pottery of Deruta. It is less easy to distinguish the style, especially from that of Siena and consequently from that of Faenza, in the smaller dishes and in the pharmacy jars. However, these last also sometimes had particularly characteristic forms, as, for example, the two-handled vase on a high spreading foot with a bulb- or baluster-shaped belly, and the goblet, also with a high foot, with straight vertical sides.

PL. 39
FIG. *xvi*
PL. 40

Together with dark blue, orange, yellow, and green, Deruta made ample use of the combination of dark blue and a metallic luster of a brassy yellow tone, with iridescent effects ranging from golden "beetle" green to violet. This combination was used by the painters for most of the thematic motifs that adorned polychrome vessels, particularly for male and female busts but also for whole figures, which reflected the style and taste of Peruginesque painting, of Pinturicchio, and the youthful Raphael.

The technique of this luster came from the Middle East and from Moorish Spain, but we do not know how it was introduced into

Italy. We suppose that some artisans brought it when they fled from Spain to avoid certain measures taken after the Christian reconquest, or it may have been brought by Corsair captives, or even, as one might infer from Ligismundo Tizio's account at Siena, through the agency of artisans purposely transferred to Spanish workshops to steal the secret. However this may have been, in Deruta the luster appears on examples dating from the very beginning of the sixteenth century, and persists there for many years.

The color combination was dark blue upon white in the design and shading, with the metallic luster in one color only. Deruta seems rarely, and then only at the beginning of this period, to have made use of ruby-red luster, as seen in the mural panel with St. Sebastian, at the Victoria and Albert Museum, dated 1501. Thus, the work of the whole school shows an austere restraint, with very little concession to the pictorial sense. The ornamentation itself rests on geometric and flower and plant patterns. Even in those examples in which a scene, religious or secular, is represented, it is treated in an obviously two-dimensional manner owing to the nature of the luster, which, not being capable of gradations of tone, does not encourage the illusion of volume or, consequently, of perspective. The glitter and iridescence of the metallic coating are, instead, effectively set off by uneven surfaces, upon which the light is reflected with widely varying incidence: this leads to the fairly frequent use of ornaments, PL. 41 such as scales, bosses, gadroons, and other more complicated designs, modeled in low relief.

Just as at Siena it has been possible to distinguish the work of the painter of Master Benedetto's plate, and that of the Nessus Painter, so in Deruta certain distinct personalities have been identified, such as that of the painter of the plate with grotesques, at the Victoria and Albert Museum, which bears the inscription *fatto in diruta* and the date 1515 or 1516, who worked in polychrome as well as in dark blue and luster. There was also

a master of Signorellian inspiration who used to scrape away the enamel in parts to obtain warm flesh tones by exposing the bare tawny color of the terracotta covered only with its transparent glaze.

Neither of these painters seems to have been responsible for the fine and complicated decoration of the pavement, dated 1524, formerly in the Church of St. Francis in Deruta, the remains of which, unfortunately much the worse for wear, are now preserved in the civic museum of that town. The variation shown in the shapes of the tiles, stars or crosses of Oriental inspiration, is further en- PL. 42 riched by the different ornamental motif of each tile, in which the knots, foliage, and arabesques on a dark-blue ground of the cross-shaped tiles alternate with the polychrome representations of stars, in which figures of saints, symbolic images, male and female busts, knights, children, boats, landscapes, and so on, are strongly drawn and painted with a harmonious sense of color.

The designs of the tiles, which, though more carefully executed, offer the same forms and colors as seen on the large figured plates, remind us now, in concluding this cycle, of the works of some decades later, some signed by Giacomo Mancini, called "the Friar" (*il Frate*), and some by Francesco Urbini, but both painted in polychrome as well as in luster.

The designs of the Friar are always well and strongly drawn. He was a man of some culture, who was in the habit of describing at length on the back of the dish the scene represented, as in the dish, dated 1545, at the Victoria and Albert Museum showing Brada- PL. 43 mante and Atlante, taken from the edition of *Orlando Furioso* produced by Giolito of Venice.

Francesco Urbini painted in polychrome and frequently enriched his output with luster of various tones. He seems to have worked also in his native city. In Deruta in 1537 he signed a round plate with Apollo and Daphne (also FIG. XVII in the same London museum) in which are noticeable, besides the strongly drawn design, certain mannerisms of shading and ornamentation.

Artisans from Montelupo were working at Cafaggiolo. The wealthy patronage of the Medici, for whom the ware seems to have been reserved, enabled the workshop to produce, in the first quarter of the sixteenth century, some of the most refined examples of Italian majolica.

We have already referred to the part played by Montelupo during the fifteenth century in what may be generically called Florentine production, and the summoning from here to the new workshops of Cafaggiolo of the artisans Stefano and Piero di Filippo, who later took the name of Fattorini, is another proof of this. Apparently the masters who were to direct the potteries at Cafaggiolo for the next hundred years all came from Montelupo. Certain peculiarities of ornamentation and certain styles and shapes of dishes bear witness to continual contacts with that center. These contacts are also revealed in the composition of the ware, wrought in clay with a very small percentage of iron. Nevertheless, the soft enamel, which frequently, especially toward the end of this period, shows a tendency to flake, and the greater emphasis on decoration, particularly of the *istoriato* style, show so many clear affinities with the art of the Faventine masters as to justify the inclusion of PL. 38 Cafaggiolo among the workshops in the sphere of Faventine influence.

The name of one painter, "Jap°" (i.e., Jacopo), appears coupled with the place indication *In Chaffaguolo* on the back of a roundel with PL. 44 Judith and her Handmaid, bearing the head of Holofernes, at the Victoria and Albert Museum. The scene is painted over the entire surface of the plate. This is the case also with the plate depicting the majolica artist painting PL. 45 a portrait of two young betrothed, now in the same museum, in which the ground, filled with sturdy dark-blue brush strokes, resembles the ground of certain Faventine examples of the end of the fifteenth century. The mark "SP,"

scribbled on the back of the plate showing the artist, which possibly stands for the Medicean motto *Semper* but which might also be the initials of the names Stefano and Piero, is in other examples coupled with the place name "Chaffaguolo" and links it with the bowl of the Damiron Collection in Lyons, which shows the story of Diana and Endymion within a border of *amorini*, or cherubs, and tritons, and also with the plate at the Victoria and Albert Museum, which bears the figure of St. George, after Donatello, also bordered with ornate grotesques. The backs of these plates are decorated with "porcelain" flower sprays or string work, and the painter shows a fondness for a dark-blue ground for the grotesques and skies, and also for certain characteristic ways of arranging or representing rocks. He paints in polychrome, yellow, ocher, blue, green, and black to which, in the older pieces, he adds a typical reddish brown. All these elements are characteristic of the painter Jacopo, to whom these four plates are attributed, together with the plate painted all over with grotesques, with a central scene of Leda and the Swan, in PL. 46 the Victoria and Albert Museum, and the bowl with the arms and devices of Pope Leo X (1513–21), at the British Museum, and many others in French, German, and English museums, variously inspired by engravings from Mantegna, Nicoletto da Modena, and Lucas van Leyden.

All these characteristics prove a precise knowledge of the working methods of the Faventine masters of the early *istoriato*, although Jacopo's work presents a more robust approach, is less given to subtlety, and does not imitate the Faventine habit of picking out highlights in a white pigment, akin to tin glaze. Jacopo instead uses the sgraffito method, which exposes the white of the enamel. This knowledge of Faventine art is matched with a taste formed by contact with great Florentine artists of the later fifteenth century, such as Donatello and, above all, Botticelli, in whose workshop Falke suggests that Jacopo learned his art.

xix

xx

xxi

xxii

xix BOWL WITH CORONATION OF CHARLES V. FAENZA, CASA PIROTA (CA. 1530). BOLOGNA, MUSEO CIVICO. *xx* BACK OF BOWL WITH CORONATION OF CHARLES V. *xxi* PLATE WITH MARTYRDOM OF ST. CECILIA. URBINO, NICOLA PELLIPARIO (1528). FLORENCE, BARGELLO. *xxii* INSCRIPTION ON BACK OF PLATE WITH MARTYRDOM OF ST. CECILIA.

xxiii

xxiv

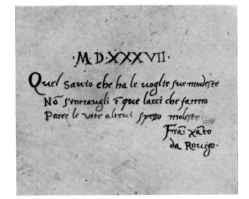

xxv

xxvi

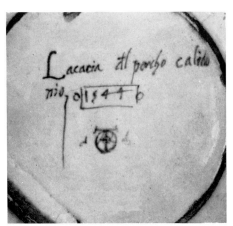

xxvii

xxiii BOWL FROM SERVICE FOR CONSTABLE OF FRANCE ANNE DE MONTMORENCY, WITH "STORY" OF JOVE AND SEMELE. URBINO, GUIDO DURANTINO (1535). LONDON, BRITISH MUSEUM. *xxiv* INSCRIPTION ON BACK OF BOWL WITH JOVE AND SEMELE. *xxv* INSCRIPTION ON BACK OF PLATE BY F. X. AVELLI, WITH CHASTITY OF JOSEPH (PL. 64). *xxvi* PLATE WITH HUNT OF CALYDONIAN BOAR. URBINO, ORAZIO FONTANA (1544). LONDON, BRITISH MUSEUM. *xxvii* BACK OF PLATE WITH HUNT OF CALYDONIAN BOAR.

Jacopo may have been the son of Stefano Fattorini, whose name appears in documents of 1522 and who was later to take over the management of the workshop but who, according to Guasti, would have been seventy years old in 1576 and therefore still a boy about 1510 when these plates were painted. Or Jacopo may have been of other descent, in which case we do not know what family name he bore or whence he came.

Another master, whom Rackham calls the Painter of Vulcan, shows some resemblances to the painter Jacopo, but has a lighter hand, a fondness for aerial perspective, and for the use of white pigment, akin to tin glaze, for highlights. These features link him much more closely with the Faventine masters, so that it is very hard to distinguish his work from theirs.

Still another hand is apparent in the plate showing Pope Leo X in Procession, in the Victoria and Albert Museum. The initials SP, sometimes coupled with the name Cafaggiolo, often appear also on ware decorated with nonfigurative designs, for the most part with dark-blue "porcelain" ornamentation, frequent-

FIG. xiii

ly including trophies, strapwork, instruments, and heraldic arms of a type which, apart from the composition of the enamel, is markedly different from similar examples of Faventine craftsmanship.

The monogram is also found on some rare pieces decorated with a brassy yellow, golden yellow or red-gold metallic luster, sometimes accompanied by dark blue. Unless these objects were wrought at Deruta and marked with some emblem distinctive to the Tuscan workshops, such as the lozenge cut crosswise, which is a mark of Faenza, they must be considered as proof that the technique of applied metallic luster had extended to many more centers than we are generally accustomed to number: to Deruta, as we have seen, and later on to Gubbio and Pesaro, as we shall see.

Zoan Maria at
Casteldurante

The painter apparently responsible for transferring to the Duchy of Urbino the methods

of the Faenza workshops is the painter of the bowl with the arms of Pope Julius II, at the Metropolitan Museum of New York (Lehman Coll.). This has on the back, in a wreath of dark-blue trailing vines, treated in a manner suggesting naturalism stiffening into arabesque, the inscription *1508 adi 12 de sete[m]br facta fu i[n] Castel dura[n]t Zoua[n] maria v[asa]ro* (made on September 12, 1508, Casteldurante, Zouan Maria, Potter).

Frontispiece

In the center is Pope Della Rovere's own emblem of the oak tree and on each side is a little wheel, one bearing the Roman abbreviation IU(lio) II. Above is a Veronica's veil, held up by a little angel, and on either side of this is a Gradual, one open and one closed. A ribbon bears the lettering IV. II. PON. MAX. TV. ES. SACERD[OS]. I[N] ETER[NUM] (Julius II, Pontifex Maximus. Thou art a priest for ever). In the lower half of the bowl are warlike trophies with the coat of arms of the Bolognese Senator Melchiorre di Giorgio Manzoli, one of the forty nominated by Pope Julius in the same year, 1508. To him must therefore be attributed the commission and the gift of the bowl. The papal arms stand out in the midst of a symmetrically arranged design of grotesques. There are two *amorini* crowned with laurel wreaths, seated on dolphins and blowing trumpets. Two more *amorini*, standing on well-filled cornucopias, seem to be holding the cords supporting the heavy festoon from which hangs the cloth of honor which forms a background for the triple tiara and keys; a couple of satyrs, also blowing trumpets, are seated on candelabra, one on either side of the dish. The scene, enriched with ribbons, smaller trophies, trailing sprays, and eagles, testifies to a horror vacui determined to break up the dark-blue ground. This dark blackish blue is the dominant tone and is combined with pale yellow and peacock yellow. The design is painted in blue and the details in green, with rare touches of manganese purple of an amethyst tone.

The colors of Zoan Maria's bowl, its typically brilliant vitreous enamel, the arrangement of the candelabra design on the blackish-blue ground, and the details of style clearly link this with a series of other examples showing the same characteristics. There are two similar plates, also dated 1508, decorated with *putti* and grotesques evidently inspired by two sections of the same engraving. One is now at the Galleria Estense in Modena, the other in the Lehman Collection at the Metropolitan Museum of New York. The technical composition common to both shows that they came from a Faventine workshop. The results of recent excavations in this important center prove that the style of Zoan Maria's bowl persisted and was further developed in Faenza itself, where it appeared also upon a comparatively late example—a plate, in the Victoria and Albert Museum, with trophies on a dark-blue ground. This plate has on the back, together with the usual circles and lozenges cut crosswise (one can see a ball cut crosswise with a dot within a quadrant, twice repeated in the above-mentioned bowl of Pope Julius II), the monogram BT, frequently found on Faventine work, both by the Master of the Resurrection, as we have seen, and by the painter known by the initials F.R., as we shall see later.

It is quite certain that Zoan Maria, or his painter, took to Casteldurante, now called Urbania, a few miles from Urbino, the whole Faventine repertory: palette, style, imaginative inventions. This repertory may be identified in works of bizarre fantasy, sometimes strongly drawn and at other times showing a more nervous stroke, in the painting of busts and *putti* framed in circles with decoration in *soprabbianco* and with rims adorned with grotesque leaves and trophies, or in complicated scenes in which *amorini*, sometimes bald-headed, play a large part. Examples may be found in the London collections of the Victoria and Albert, British, and Wallace Museums, in the Ashmolean in Oxford, in the Österreichisches Museum für Kunst und Industrie in Vienna, as well as in the catalogues of the Zschille Collection of Prague and the Pringsheim Collection of Munich, now dispersed, and the Museums of Bologna and Faenza. All these models were to inspire the work of Nicola Pellipario of Casteldurante. A few years younger than Zoan Maria, Pellipario was to develop this style in a masterly way and transfer it to another clime.

Niculoso Francisco at Seville

The vigorous, widespread influence of the early *istoriato*, the gaiety of its color, and the freedom of its fantasy reached Spain, the home of a great majolica tradition, where, through the work of the Italian Niculoso Francisco in Seville, it established itself at the very beginning of the sixteenth century and developed along the traditional lines of Moorish design. In the Church of S. Ana de Triana is the panel for the tomb of Inigo Lopez, dated 1503, with the figure of the deceased lying with his arms crossed over his stomach and his head resting on a cushion, within a border of flowery sprays interspersed with lettering. In the Church of the Convent of S. Paula is a doorway with a wide pointed arch, covered with *azulejos* adorned with grotesques in blue and white and details in other colors, which serve as a background for six medallions with figures of saints and one, in the keystone, representing the birth of Christ, all modeled in low relief and colored in the Della Robbia manner. Inside and outside the arch are angels, heraldic arms and devices, and cartouches with the name NICULOSO. PISANO. and the precise marking NICULOSO FRANCISCO ITALIANO ME FECIT INELAGNO DEI 15. 4. (N.F. the Italian made me in the year of Our Lord 1504). In the same year, 1504, was set up the altarpiece of the Alcazar in which, within a sumptuous border of grotesques and candelabra, interspersed with busts of prophets and patriarchs, is painted a central scene of the Visitation, while on the frontal the Annunciation is enclosed in a wreath supported by griffins. Both these works are clearly inspired by Spanish-Flemish painting.

In 1518 Niculoso, who died before July, 1529, signed works in the Church of Tentudia in the Estremadura. His activity, mostly shown in mural panels, showed his swift adaptation to the taste of the country, and seems to have brought him wealth, which proves how much his new art was prized. As for the description "Pisan," which is sometimes used with, or instead of, "Italian," it must be remembered that, although it might also indicate an artist's place of origin, it was generally used in Spain as a specification of a man's art. The ships that carried the coastal trade in the Western Mediterranean and brought to Italian shores the name *maiolica* for products of Spanish origin took back to Spain the name *pisa* for those of Italian origin, so that in Spain *Pisano* meant the same as the later *maiolicaro* in Central and Northern Italy, and *faenzaro* in the South and in France.

We notice here, in passing, that the transference of artisans, models, and methods of work had turned toward Hungary by the end of the fifteenth century, to the court of that Humanist Prince Matthias Corvin and, by the beginning of the sixteenth century, toward France and Flanders. Throughout the course of this century, the presence and influence of Italian craftsmen were obvious in these two last-named countries. The first documents to mention French localities date from the end of the fifteenth century and the first years of the sixteenth; in Flanders, at Antwerp, Guido di Savino of Casteldurante, alias Guido Andries, appeared at least as early as 1510.

Influence of engravings and prints The *istoriato* decoration inevitably resulted in the regional schools of painting exercising a more or less decided influence over the ceramic artists. Majolica is not the ideal field for pictorial expression, since it must make full use of plastic elements, such as the form of the receptacles, and elements of color and substance (the clay and enamel). The material of which the vase or the plate is formed is an integral part of the style, and the style springs from the appropriate use of the potters' material. It is true that the utilitarian, practical function of the ceramic vessel was tending, at the beginning of the sixteenth century and particularly after the appearance of the *istoriato* style, to give way to the need to give visual enjoyment. This tendency certainly led to a greater, indeed an exaggerated, concentration on the decoration, to the neglect of the form, at least until around the middle of the century. Nevertheless, these principles of the strict relation between style and material, never entirely forgotten, preserved for majolica its own peculiar character.

However, the field of figure painting in which the majolica painters were now at work exposed them to the influence of the schools of painting nearest to them or most akin to them in temperament. Thus, in the work of Jacopo at Cafaggiolo we have seen traces of Botticellian influence or forms reminiscent of other Florentine masters; at Deruta we see reflections of the art of Perugino, Pinturicchio, and the youthful Raphael; at Faenza echoes of the Bolognese artists, of Viti, Aspertini, and Ripanda, followers of Francia, of Signorelli and Melozzo and of the local studio of Giambattista Bertucci, who in his turn was affected by the Umbrian school, and of other studios of the Romagna. We have already mentioned the influence of Flemish and Catalan painters in the art of Niculoso, who called himself an Italian, though working in Spain.

These assimilations of manner and subject were tremendously encouraged by the use of engravings and prints, which were becoming more widely distributed. Their effect was felt, obviously, not merely in the imitation of forms but also in the methods of expression, which the potters assimilated and then re-created by their own means: enamel and color. The range is wide: from the crude Florentine workers in *niello* of the fifteenth century, the designers of tarot cards, the woodcuts of the first incunabula printed in Venice, the tentative compositions in the grotesque manner and the masters of Northern and Central Italy to the great German engravers and the Raphaelesque school led by Marcantonio. It is unnecessary to quote examples. The works of the

Faventine masters of the early *istoriato* amply reveal their contacts not only in Italy but also with foreign artists. These contacts were perhaps made first for purposes of trade, through which they acquired the Bavarian azure blue, but were increased by other agencies, including the presence of students from Northern lands at the Studium of Bologna. On the other hand, the diffusion of German prints in Italy was very widespread—the Germans being much attracted by the spiritual climate of the peninsula.

The stile bello at Faenza The period described as that of the *stile bello*, or "beautiful style," which lasted until nearly the middle of the sixteenth century, was brought to its climax by masters belonging to a younger generation than those who initiated the *istoriato*.

In Faenza this second generation, led by the painter represented by the initials F.R., by the artists of the Pirotti, Bergantini, and Manara workshops, and by the "Green Man," is characterized by the widespread habit of painting on a gray-blue enamel glaze instead of on white.

The lavender-gray ground, *bertino*, *berettino*, as it is called in the old documents, apparently also derives again from Middle Eastern prototypes, probably from Persia, but possibly from Syria or Egypt. It may even have been inspired by a glaze, Hellenistic or Roman, admired in some church treasury, unearthed in excavations, or imitated from the glass-workers of Murano. A mural roundel in the Victoria and Albert Museum in London, of an intense dark-blue enamel, adorned with the Sacred Initials of St. Bernardino's device, YHS, within a white and orange rayed border, and with the date 1491 accompanied by the initials MI and CA surmonted by a cross (possibly a Carthusian emblem) may serve to indicate the moment of its introduction. The intense dark-blue enamel is generally enlivened by threadlike white decorations of Renaissance inspiration; the enamel of a paler tint, more like an ash or pearl gray, offers an ideal chromatic base for figurative ornamentation and for borders of grotesques, reserved in white and with white pigment for the highlights, upon a ground filled in with dark-blue brush strokes.

The successful gray-blue-white combination, enriched in the *istoriato* style with the compound colors yellow, orange, and green, and occasionally with manganese purple, was a characteristic feature of the Faventine workshops, and was to be repeated in the Veneto and Rome, where foliage decoration, easily and rapidly wrought, soon spread, since a numerous colony of potters from Faenza and other centers was busily at work there. PL. 52

The threadlike decoration on dark enamel and the polychrome decoration on lavender gray have in common some embellishments which the sixteenth-century documents call *gentilezze e vaghezze*, or refinements and embellishments, consisting of coiled sprays, arabesques, leaves, interlacing, bunches of fruit, trophies, and so on, all giving the decoration an excuse to enliven with color the pale azure ground on which the most outstanding feature was a festoon of leaves and fruit encircling the outer edge of the rim. In this type of ornament we find the most highly developed use of color by the artists of the Faventine school. Those masters now revealed the intrinsic possibilities of color on majolica and gave them absolute values, of the same importance as plastic values, derived until then from form alone. Enamel revealed in full one of its supreme qualities: color. The love of color, always noticeable in the masters of Faenza, at times led to the use of yellow or green grounds, generally with dark blue, and occasionally with the addition of harmonizing colors. PL. 51

The documents in the archives that refer to the brothers Matteo, Negro, Gianlorenzo, and Gianfrancesco, sons of Pirotto Paterni (Paterini), the managers of the largest and, so far as we know, the most famous sixteenth-century workshop, the Casa Pirota, show that the peak period of their activity was between

1505 and 1528, when the *pestis magna* (Great Plague), which destroyed a quarter of the population of Faenza, dealt a grave blow to the brothers' business with the sudden death of Matteo, Gianlorenzo, and Gianfrancesco. Negro survived them but for only three years.

The documentation that refers to the brothers Pietro and Paolo Bergantini, who directed another large workshop in the early sixteenth century, is restricted to the years between 1503, or possibly 1497, and 1558; that referring to the brothers Giuliano and Sebastiano Manara deals with the years between 1489 and 1549. Other documents speak of the Viani, the Gubadinos, the Gulmanelli, and many more.

The commercial shrewdness and professional ability of the masters brought prosperity to these workshops. Within these shops labored, perhaps somewhat erratically as they probably alternated this work with other activity (the decoration of dowry chests and birth trays, the illumination of books, and mural and panel pictures), certain painters who do not seem to have been closely or exclusively bound to any one shop and thus added to the confusion of styles which had already, for obvious reasons, invaded the whole field of ceramic modeling and decoration.

PLS. 48, 49, 50 The Monogrammist F.R. was responsible for a series of works, not all marked, which show him progressing from the first tentative manner of the early *istoriato* to the fullness of Raphaelesque forms and features, which were taken largely from engravings distributed by Marcantonio and then painted in polychrome, rich in compound colors, upon both white and lavender-gray enamel. The design, which was at first, about 1522, threadlike and faltering, became gradually more sturdy and decided, and acquired a style which sometimes leads to confusion with the work of Avelli, of whom more will be said later. Some marks, such as the lozenge cut crosswise—the distinguishing if not the exclusive mark of the Casa Pirota—on the back of the plate with a rather enigmatic scene,

xxviii TRENCHER WITH HERALDIC ARMS AND GROTESQUES ON "BERETTINO" BLUE-GRAY ENAMEL. FAENZA, CASA PIROTA (1528-36). FAENZA MUSEUM.

musicians, a woman, *putti*, and a landscape, accompanied by the initials BT (which, as we have said, occur also on works by the Master of the Resurrection), lead one to suppose that F.R. was a wandering, and therefore an independent, craftsman.

The "Green Man" was the author of some vessels decorated with figures on lavender-gray enamel in which the distinguishing characteristic is a greenish shading, produced also by faint yellow washes over the dark blue of the ground, and also by the artist's habit of indicating backgrounds with sloping mountains by means of accentuated convexity, as in the bowl with heraldic arms, dated 1526, in the Galleria Estense of Modena, showing a vague allegorical scene, or in another bowl, dated 1527, now at the Petit Palais of Paris, portraying the Fall of Phaëthon.

The Painter of the Bergantini Bowl is so called because of the indication on a bowl with polychrome decoration on lavender-gray enamel in a private collection in Paris, dated 1529. This bowl is adorned front and back with trophies, grotesques, and busts with shields, which serve as a border for the story of Marcus Curtius casting himself into the

41

chasm. This example shows the influence of Signorelli, seen also in a fairly compact group of works, dating from the years 1524–35, once generically attributed by Fortnum to the above-mentioned "Green Man," but now considered to constitute a family on their own, although it is not easy to distinguish them from works by that master.

A bowl with David and Goliath, at the Victoria and Albert Museum, painted at Forlì between 1520 and 1530, some plates and the PL. 47 small bowl with the School of Athens, at the Museo Civico of Arezzo, with the date 1524 set within the quarters of the circle cut crosswise (generally considered to be a mark of the Casa Pirota) are also indicative of a wandering craftsman. The painter of the bowl FIG. xix with the Coronation of Charles V, in the Museo Civico of Bologna, presumably made in 1530 or immediately after, marked on the back with the inscription in dark-blue capital FIG. xx letters FATO IN FAENZA IN CAXA PIROTA (made in Faenza in the Pirota workshop) surrounded by a border of grotesques sketchily drawn in orange, has been identified by some with the painter of the initials F.R. In the same workshop anonymous decorators were developing, with varied fantasy, the ornamentation with grotesques on a dark-blue ground or monochrome decoration on laven- FIG. xxviii der-gray enamel or polychrome on white enamel, a decoration that usually serves as a border for the central design of the well: a heraldic device, a *putto* or some other figure. In the most mature phase of the *stile bello* these same anonymous painters split up the constituent elements of grotesque ornamentation, by now reduced to a sort of code—dolphins, cornucopias, foliage, circular shields with trumpets, and so on—and rearranged PL. 53 them in compartments, speckled in various tones, to accentuate the breaking up of the formerly smooth surface. This breaking up had already taken place in the plastic field, in imitation of the much-admired *repoussé* vessels of precious metal. The fondness for uneven, sometimes riotously uneven, surfaces,

is now expressed in the invention of the *crespina*, a round bowl on a foot, embossed, gadrooned, or molded in the form of shells, masks, etc.—a development that proves the exhaustion of pictorial expression and prepares the way for the revolutionary *bianchi*, or white ware, of Faenza.

Last in order of time, in Faenza, in this period which may be called that of the second *istoriato*, came the painter Baldassare Manara. His dated works belong to the fourth decade of the century. An unmarked plate with Procne and Philomela, formerly in the Harris Collection of London, dates from 1532. To 1534 belong the plates with the Vestal Virgin Tuccia and with Narcissus, belonging to the same service adorned with heraldic arms, now at the British Museum and the Victoria and Albert, and those with Atalanta and Hippomenes and with the Death of Hesperia, formerly in the Pringsheim Collection. To 1535 belong the bowls with two versions of the Resurrection of Christ (one of which is signed PL. 54 with the name in full: Baldasara Manara), at the Victoria and Albert and in the Wallace Collection in London. Of the year 1536 is the roundel with the equestrian figure of the Condottiere Battistone Castellini, at the British Museum, which bears on the back the lengthy inscription *Mile cinque cente t[r]enta sei adj tri de luje. Baldasara manara faentine faciebat* (July 3, 1536, Baldassare Manara of Faenza made it). We may assume that Manara was working until the middle of the century, thus joining forces with a group of other masters of whom we shall speak later. Nevertheless, one can see a resemblance to works of the painter whose initials are G.I., whom he to some extent imitated. In other mannerisms and pictorial details, Manara, who may also have worked for some time away from his own town, showed a knowledge of the art of Pellipario, and offered most conclusive evidence of the extreme receptivity of the majolica painters and of the mutual influence exercised by masters and workshops and different centers.

FIG. xxi

FIG. xxii

In Casteldurante the master who carried on the Faventine manner of Zoan Maria was, as we have already said, Nicola del Pellicciaio, or Pellipario. He was born about the year 1475, and his mark, a monogram woven of the letters forming his name Nicolò, may be seen on a bowl with the figure of an Emperor enthroned, dated 1521, at the Hermitage in Leningrad, and upon a fragment showing Mount Parnassus, at the Louvre. A large plate showing the Martyrdom of St. Cecilia, which is at the Bargello in Florence, also bears the monogram and the inscription *Jhistoria de Sancta Cicilia la qualle è Fata in botega de Guido da Castello durante Jn Urbino 1528* (Story of St. Cecilia made in the workshop of Guido da Casteldurante in Urbino 1528). His full name, Nicola da U(rbino), is instead drawn on a bowl, with the Sacrifice to Diana, at the British Museum.

This large plate, painted by Nicola in the year 1528 in the workshop of his son Guido, whom he declares to be a native of Casteldurante, might also indicate his own origin, and might also mean that the painter had no workshop of his own. His manner, as seen in a shallow bowl at the Hermitage in Leningrad, with the *Vergine della Scala* and the date 1527, together with the name of the city of Fabriano in a border of lozenges cut crosswise, and the indication *da Urbino* beside the name on the bowl at the British Museum, might be held to confirm this supposition, even if we excluded from his *œuvre* the bowl at Sèvres, with Arion riding on a Dolphin and the name of the city of Ravenna.

Nicola was also the author of some *credenze*, or table services. Of the first of these, which we consider was made about 1515, there remain seventeen pieces at the Correr Museum in Venice and three pieces in museums abroad. Since one of these, the plate in the Rijksmuseum at Amsterdam, bears on the rim the coat of arms of the Ridolfi impaling Medici, the service, which is generally known by the name of the Venetian museum, has been described by Falke as the Ridolfi

service. The painting, executed with the tip of the brush, in dominant dark blue with gradations of amethyst and some few compound colors, brings the Pellipario of this period nearer to the Master of the Resurrection. The narrative scenes, mostly drawn from traditional love stories and freely composed after woodcuts from the Venetian incunabula, are set in open landscapes, showing that the painter, who had a marked sense of tridimensionality, was attracted by the art of Giorgione.

A few years later in date are three more services. One of these was probably made about 1519 for Isabella d'Este, recently widowed by the death of Gianfrancesco Gonzaga, as is shown by her armorial bearings and the many devices she adopted. The second service is adorned with still unidentified arms, with a ladder and a banner. The third has a shield *tiercé en bande* with three augers, possibly of the Gualtierotti of Florence. In these three services, and especially in Isabella's of which we can trace twenty-five pieces, Nicola's style remains refined and preserves certain mannerisms, such as figures with tiny faces and slender bodies full of feminine grace, Greek noses, *putti* with long slim sinewy bodies, limbs (especially the lower limbs) tapering at the joints, spiral clouds, rocks shaped like stalagmites and stalactites, trees with wavy trunks, delicately drawn landscapes, deep and wide. The palette reveals, on the contrary, a more emphatic use of color: the compound colors are more clearly defined and the dominant blue yields to a greater chromatic equilibrium. The harmony between form and ornament is almost always carefully preserved. Only the flat plates have scenes painted all over them. Hollow dishes have the bowl adorned with heraldic arms, flanked by *putti*, sometimes framed in a wide wreath decorated in *bianco soprabbianco*, and the "story" is painted around the rim. In the Correr service the little scenes painted on the bowl are likewise distinguished from those around the rim. The

Gualtierotti service is an exception to this rule. Nicola, the painter, does not like hollow dishes or vases, because they do not offer him a flat surface that he can use to create illusions of space. The only example of his vase painting known to us is on a ewer belonging to Isabella's service, reproduced by Delange, formerly in the Rothschild Collection in Paris, which is decorated solely with grotesques —a style known to have been used occasionally by Nicola. The "stories" of the Este-Gonzaga service do not seem to illustrate any particular theme; for the most part they are PL. 55 drawn from mythology, sometimes with repeated and varied interpretations of the same episode, but they include also stories from the Bible and from the history of Rome.

Different in color scheme from the others is a shallow bowl, at the Louvre, with Isaac PL. 56a and Rebecca observed by Abimelech, a composition taken from Raphael's Bible illustrations in the Vatican and treated by Nicola in two dominant colors, yellow and blue. Another similar bowl in the Louvre bears a PL. 56b Triumph of Death, after an engraving of a picture by Schongauer, painted in green and blue. This does not belong to the same service as the Isaac and Rebecca bowl, although closely related to it, not only in shape but also in the architectural background and the sobriety of color.

The above-mentioned large plate of 1528 with St. Cecilia, at the Bargello in Florence, which might belong to the period when Nicola established himself in Urbino, marks the transition of his art to a second phase, characterized by warmer tones, which now predominate. In this second period which ended with his death between the years 1542 and 1545, Nicola achieved a freedom of form and breadth of modeling unknown before. The forms of his figures tended to expand, as if intolerant of reality; the color gradations became harsher. Illustrative of this second period is the table service for Isabella's son, Federico Gonzaga, Duke of Mantua, and his wife Margherita Paleologo, which Nicola

painted between 1531, the year of their marriage, and 1540, the year of Federico's death. The pieces known to us, in the British Museum and the Wallace Collection in London and at the Faenza Museum, show compositions celebrating single divinities— Mars, Juno, and others—in triumphal chariots, derived possibly from cartoons by Giulio Romano, and the Council of Apollo and Minerva, always covering the entire surface of the dish, and ignoring the two different planes of the bowl and rim. Other plates with various scenes bear, in isolation, the Paleologo arms or Federico's Olympian device, set off from the rest of the decoration, and indicate a continual contact between the master and the Gonzagas.

Pellipario was naturally not only a painter of table services and *istoriato* plates, like that with the Presentation of the Virgin in the PL. 57 Temple, in the Museo Civico at Bologna, in which he used *grisaille*, and which Master Giorgio da Gubbio enriched with luster in 1532. It was largely because of Pellipario's decisive contribution that the widely diffused ornamentation with trophies and grotesques, introduced into the Duchy of Urbino by Zoan Maria, was now enriched with arabesques, *cerquate*, or wreaths of oak leaves, and *bianco* PLS. 59, 60, 61 *soprabbianco* decoration; Pellipario was largely responsible for the appearance of the "Fair Lady" series, that is, of dishes generally decorated with a single female bust, with shading in ivory or greenish *grisaille*, painted in PL. 58 reserve on a dark-blue background, with a scroll bearing the name of the lady portrayed, and the description *bella*. These dishes, which revived and adapted to the Humanistic taste a style seen in Athenian vases of the fifth century, were warmly received and enjoyed wide diffusion.

The activity of Pellipario, and the impulse he gave to figurative and abstract decoration in the two neighboring centers of Casteldurante and Urbino, encouraged many followers and imitators. From Casteldurante came the painter of the two vases in the British Museum and the Victoria and Albert Museum, decorated in 1519 with the typical monster with a serpent's body, in the workshop of Sebastiano di Marforio. Also from Casteldurante came the master who, between 1524 and 1530, dated bowls adorned with religious and secular images and scenes in which not only the coloring but a certain formal manner also are reminiscent of Nicola—so much so that this painter has been called the "pseudo-Pellipario." There were also in Urbino, Nicola's son Guido and his nephew Orazio, who, together with his brothers and sons, assumed the name Fontana. Their work leads us to the second half of the century and to Francesco Xanto Avelli.

Guido, owner of the workshop in which Nicola painted the Martyrdom of St. Cecilia, is the author of well-known plates dispersed in collections in England, France, and America, all from the same table service painted in 1535 for the Constable of France, Anne de Montmorency, whose arms they bear. In France, Montmorency, a great enthusiast for Italian art, employed and protected Masseot Abaquesne of Rouen, who designed the pavement of his château at Ecouen in 1542, and that restless artist, Bernard Palissy. The dishes of this table service, which clearly show the influence of Nicola's art, have on the back a written description of the "story" represented, and the inscription: *In la botega de M. Guido durantino jn Urbino 1535* (In the workshop of M. Guido from Durante in Urbino 1535), written in elegant characters that resemble Nicola's. The same inscription and date appear upon a plate at Sèvres with the story of Joseph sold by his Brethren, which has noticeably elongated figures and the arms of Cardinal Duprat. The same inscription also occurs on an undated bowl with the Judgment of Paris, now at Chantilly.

Giulio da Urbino may also have worked in Guido's workshop. It was he who, in 1535, painted at Rimini, in the workshop of Master Alessandro, the large jug with Scylla and Minos, in the Museo Civico in Bologna, and probably also a small group of smooth bowls, now in London, Paris, and Leningrad, which bear only the date 1535 and the place name, Rimini. In the painted scenes on these bowls, besides the elongated lines of the figures, there is the characteristic representation of walls by means of an arrangement of little strokes which resemble musical notation.

Francesco Xanto Avelli certainly seems to have been the most prolific and talented of the followers of Nicola Pellipario. He was careful to sign his works with his own name, sometimes written in full and sometimes reduced to the initials or an emblem. Born at Rovigo at the beginning of the century, he appeared in Urbino about the year 1530, and added the name of this city, where he married and established a home, to his signature on works painted up to the year 1534. Later works, which are dated up to the year 1542, no longer bear the indication *in Urbino*. Among his first dated works are a panel with St. Sebastian and St. Roch, at the Victoria and Albert Museum, dated 1528; a pilgrim's bottle with Psyche and Olympus, in the Walters Art Gallery of Baltimore, dated 1530; a pap cup, at the Correr Museum of Venice, and a plate with the Allegory of the New Year, marked *F.X.A.R. in Urbino* with the date 1530 on the back and MDXXXI on the front. In all these the artist already showed himself an expert and mature worker in majolica, which leads us to assume that, before he came to Urbino, he may have worked in other centers, possibly in Ferrara, capital of the duchy where he was born, and possibly in Faenza. The manner of these first examples is very like that of Pellipario, and like this painter he seems never to have had a workshop of his own, at least until 1542, the year in which he gathered together some workmen to assist him. One plate bears the indication of the workshop of a Francesco di Silvano in Urbino.

The "stories" are derived from engravings, mostly from those of Marcantonio, as in the plate at the Victoria and Albert Museum with the Marriage of Alexander and Roxana and the Gonzaga-Paleologo arms, or from Marco Dente, or others. Sometimes Avelli copied the original arrangement and sometimes he freely selected single figures which he used over and over again in the most varied manner, sometimes changing the clothing so as to represent different personages—so that we may assume the use of cartoons or pounced tracing papers. A hard outline gives solidity

PL. 64 to the single figures. His palette, dominated by warm lively colors, is very varied, includ-
PL. 65 ing dark blue, yellow, reddish or brownish orange, coppery and olive green, manganese purple, black, and white. Frequently, as in the work of Pellipario and other masters, the colors of the stuffs and robes fade in tone from dark blue to turquoise or violet, and from orange to yellow.

Avelli was a man of culture, and something of a poet as he shows in the manuscript entitled *Il rovere vittorioso* (The victorious oak) in the Vatican Library, and in a series of sonnets dedicated in 1537 to Francesco Maria della Rovere, Duke of Urbino, with whom he seems to have been on familiar terms. He nearly always made a note, on the back of
FIG. XXV his plates or rectangular panels, of the source of his inspiration: Virgil, Ovid, Livy, Valerius Maximus, Trogus Pompey, the Bible, and even Petrarch and Ariosto, sometimes quoting *terzine* or *quartine* more or less freely interpreted or translated. He was also interested in the historical events of his own day, which he illustrates and comments upon in inscriptions such as this: *Nell'anno de le tribulazioni de Italia; Clemente in Castel chiuso et Roma langue; Di tua discordia, Italia, il premio or hai; Fra l'arme e il fuoco stei dal XX al XXX, Italia* (In the year of Italy's tribulation; Clement imprisoned in Castello while Rome languishes; Of your disunity, Italy, you now reap the reward; You are given over to fire and sword, Italy from XX to XXX).

His vast *œuvre*, which consists of hundreds of examples dispersed in the ceramic collections of every land, contains some examples

evidently intended to form part of a series, such as the tiles with the Persian "stories," or the table services of the years 1532–33, embellished with the arms of patrons, such as the Gonfaloniere Pucci, or Jacopo Pesaro, the Bishop of Paphos, 1535, and with those of many other unidentified patrons, like those shown on the service with Samson and the Lion, made between 1531 and 1532.

Considerations of chronology and of contacts among the various workshops now bring us to Master Giorgio da Gubbio who, apart from the fact that he may or may not have painted majolica in the second firing, or *gran fuoco*, was renowned for possessing the still jealously guarded secret of luster, which he applied with skill and frequently with commendable restraint, both on work prepared in his shop and on pieces from other workshops. Sometimes these had been painted by eminent artists before Master Giorgio adorned them with brilliant iridescent tones of ruby red, gold and silver, inscribing them on the back with his mark "M.G.," with or without the place indication "Ugubio."

Master Giorgio di Pietro Andreoli was born at Intra on Lake Maggiore between 1465 and 1470, and moved from Pavia to Gubbio about the year 1490, together with his brothers Giovanni and Salimbene. In 1498 he was granted citizenship in Gubbio by the Duke of Urbino, who for twenty years exempted him from paying taxes and duties and appointed him lord of that citadel. In 1519 Pope Leo X renewed the exemptions, without any restriction of time, for this "excellent Master of the art of majolica," that is, of the art of luster.

Master Giorgio was the director of a flourishing pottery and was treated as a privileged person "in consideration of the honor which redounds to the city, to his overlords, and to the community from the popularity of those wares, in whatever land they are taken, and in consideration of their great usefulness and profitableness in revenue." He died in Gubbio about the year 1553. In 1547 his sons had

Giorgio da Gubbio

46

drawn up a contract binding each other to carry on their father's workshop, dividing the various tasks, with Cencio responsible for producing all kinds of pottery *ad usum boni magistri* (as a good master potter) and Ubaldo devoting himself to painting, and employing painters, and, as they said, "filling," that is, completing the painted vases with *maiolica*, that is, with luster *ubi opus fuerit*, where it was needed. Their father had already called in collaborators from various places, most of all from the neighboring center of Casteldurante, for the decoration of plates and vases. It is to this varied collaboration that Gubbio owes the eclectic character of its ornamentation, which found its unifying element and also its principal *raison d'être* in the application of metallic luster.

Master Giorgio and those who carried on his work produced, like the Deruta artists, pieces with relief ornamentation, such as bowls with raised figures, arms, monograms, or medallions surrounded by rayed borders,

PL. 68   gadroons and bosses which offered uneven surfaces upon which the iridescent gleams were reflected according to the varying incidence of the light.

We have referred to the obviously Oriental origin of the technique, which Master Giorgio seems to have begun using in the second decade of the sixteenth century if we consider as one of his first examples the dish dated 1518 at the Museum in Arezzo, with the Aldobrandini arms set between grotesques and *putti* in the manner of Casteldurante, which shows a dark blue and a sober green allied to the warm gold and ruby-red tones characteristic of the master's palette.

Differing in this from the Oriental usage and from that of the Deruta workshops, Master Giorgio also used luster to add color to vessels which, even when specially prepared to be finished in luster, were never limited to monochrome or to the blue-gold color scheme predominant in the East and faithfully imitated in Deruta. They were, instead, enriched with at least two colors "of

xxix INSCRIPTION BY MASTER GIORGIO DA GUBBIO ON BACK OF N. PELLIPARIO'S PLATE WITH PRESENTATION OF VIRGIN IN TEMPLE (PL. 57).

the second firing" (*a gran fuoco*), dark blue and green upon a white enamel, together with the red and gold (which, when very thickly applied, assumed the colder tones of silver), which were added in the iridescent metallic luster. The pictorial fantasy and the lively riotous sense of color, which induced the master to take elaborate examples already adorned with figures and glowing with color   PL. 66 and to enrich them still further, sharply distinguished the art of Gubbio from the more restrained art of Deruta which preceded it and remained as its contemporary.

Some examples that demonstrate this character are of such rare excellence as to place the master on a lofty artistic plane. There are, for example, the bowl of the year 1525, with the figure of St. Jude, in the Museo   PL. 67 Civico of Pesaro, and the plate with the Presentation of the Virgin, in the Museo Civico of Bologna, dated 1532, in which the luster, although used very liberally as in the decoration of the bowl, is in perfect accord with the harmonies of Pellipario. Indeed, it appears to enhance them and to add its own delightful note.

Because of this metallic luster, the name

FIG. XXIX

maiolica, originally used for the wares introduced into Italy from Spain, which were enriched with this much-prized iridescent color, was now in general use in the potters' shops. Master Giorgio himself, writing on the back of the above-mentioned Bolognese plate, made it clear that his own share of the work had been limited to enriching it with "the majolica colors" (*fini de maiolica*), that is, with gold and ruby red.

Cavaliere Cipriano Piccolpasso of Casteldurante, in a manuscript which he wrote about the years 1556–57, possibly at the suggestion of Cardinal De Tournon, Bishop of Lyons, who was a guest of the Duke of Urbino at Casteldurante, left the most exhaustive technical treatise on the art of the potters of his time, divided into three books. Here he confirms the use of this term and its precise meaning.

In the second book, after having described the method of preparing enamels, glazes, and colors, and indicated the quantities required, he writes: "I do not intend to proceed any further until I have told you about *maiolica*, from what I have heard from others, not that I have ever made it nor even seen it made." The process, entrusted to the skilled potters, was kept a close secret. "I do know that it is painted on finished ware. This I have seen in Gubbio in the house of a Master Cencio of that place" (the son of Master Giorgio), "and they follow this method in painting it. They leave unpainted those places where it is to be applied, not coloring them in any way. For example, when they draw on a little plate an arabesque of this kind" (here he draws a design) "or rather a grotesque, these leaves, which would properly be colored green, are left blank, and only the outlines are drawn. The ware is finally fired, like the others, then, when it has been fired, these blanks are filled with *maiolica*, which is made in this way." Here Piccolpasso gives the recipe for red luster and gold luster, with a minute description of the ingredients, the quantities and the method of preparation, the firing, the method of building the furnace, "which is as different from the others as is the method of setting the kiln and of painting. . . . You must know that these chambers are small—for example, 3 feet in every direction, or 4—and this comes about because the art is so uncertain that frequently out of a hundred pieces barely six are good. It is true that the art is esentially beautiful and ingenious and when the works are good they are paid for in gold. Only three colors are used: gold, silver, and red. If anyone wants another color he must apply it before the second firing, always leaving the spaces for the *maiolica*." Later on, toward the end of the sixteenth century, at the same time as the term *faïence* came into wide use in France, the word *maiolica* was to widen its meaning, as we shall see, and to indicate first the enamel coating and then the whole enameled product without the luster enrichment, which fell into disuse.

In Urbino the sons of Guido Durantino or Fontana, and particularly Orazio, continued to work, first in their father's workshop and then, after 1565, in a separate workshop. During this time they perfected the technique of the *istoriato* ornamentation in rich polychrome, which was now accompanied by Raphaelesque fantasies.

The monogram of Orazio Fontana, who died in 1571, appears on a small group of dated plates, seven of which, spanning the period between 1541 and 1544, may be described here. The first, dated 1541, at the Victoria and Albert Museum, shows a Race of Horsemen beyond the walls of Urbino, the city's name appearing, with the painter's monogram, on the back. The second, in the Schlossmuseum of Berlin, shows the contest between the Muses and the Pierides; the monogram appears on the front, and on the back is the mark of the shop of Orazio's father, Guido, and the date 1542. The third and fourth, with the monogram and the date 1543 on the back, are preserved at the Fabre Museum of Montpellier and at the Österreichisches Museum für Angewandte Kunst in Vienna, and

48

FIGS. xxvi, xxvii

PLS. 69, 70
FIG. XXX

represent, respectively, two episodes from the Trojan War, one the Rape of Helen, derived indirectly from Raphael through the well-known engraving by Marcantonio, and the other a battle scene, after a Raphaelesque composition. Three others, which also have the monogram on the back with the date 1544, are preserved in the Chigi Zondadari Collection in Siena, at the British Museum, and in the Museum of Decorative Arts in Budapest. The Chigi plate, with the Rape of the Sabine Women, recalls the style of the plate with the Muses and Pierides; the second, with the Hunt of the Calydonian Boar, is more in the manner of Francesco Durantino, who in the same year, 1544, signed a plate, also in the British Museum, portraying the story of Coriolanus; the third, with Neptune, reveals a technique more decided, vigorous, and vibrant.

From the workshop of Orazio Fontana came the great table service ornamented with "stories" and Raphaelesques, commissioned by Duke Guidobaldo II. Part of it is in the Bargello in Florence, having come from the holdings of the Medici, who had inherited it, and part of it is now in the Victoria and Albert Museum. The equipment of the ducal pharmacy was given to the Sanctuary of the Holy House at Loreto by Duke Francesco Maria II at the beginning of the seventeenth century. Its vessels are painted with figures of apostles and prophets, and with episodes from sacred history, the history of Greece and Rome, and from mythology.

Undoubtedly the pottery of Orazio and his workshop mark the culminating period of the *virtuosismo* of the Urbinate schools. In them we see perfection of workmanship, a brilliant glaze covering the painted surfaces, a palette of rich, harmonious colors in which black, flesh color, and greens of various shades are mingled with the fundamental tints, often superimposed to create an even wider range of color. In the skillful designs and compositions sometimes laden with figures, we may safely assume the hand of some famous artists, as well as the inspiration of well-known engravings.

The incipient Baroque taste seen in forms either modeled—statuettes, groups, inkstands, saltcellars—or thrown—large dishes, wine coolers, jars, flasks, and amphoras with serpent handles—which recall in their divisions the *stucchi* of the Ducal Palace, gives these objects a festive and floridly ornate air. The Raphaelesque designs are no longer grotesques derived from engravings and therefore no longer have the customary dark ground of the first decades of the century, but are now derived from the mural paintings which the school of Raphael had widely diffused. The artist intensifies the white enamel ground, which does not afford sufficient contrast with the minute colored fantasies, by brushing in a white pigment obtained from tin.

PL. 71

The painter Francesco Durantino was a contemporary of Orazio. In 1544 he signed the already mentioned Coriolanus plate, at the British Museum, which was painted with a somewhat faltering and threadlike design in subdued tones of blue, yellow, orange, two shades of green, black, and white. In 1546 he initialed a fragment with the Death of Polyxena, bearing the mark "Urbino," now at the National Museum of Stockholm. From 1553, however, he seems to have established himself at Monte Bagnolo near Perugia. Also contemporary were Orazio's brother, Camillo Fontana, the painter of the dish with the allegory of Truth rescued by Time, at the Victoria and Albert Museum, the painter of the Myths in Modern Dress, and the painter of the service with the arms of a Cardinal of the Della Rovere house.

A family that came to the fore in Urbino in the last quarter of the century (some of its members were still working in the following century) was that of the Patanazzi, who seem to have carried on the work of the Fontana. Its members used the somewhat stale *istoriato* and Raphaelesque ornamentation, with a greater rigidity of treatment, with the increased use of a brownish orange, and with a

PL. 72

FIG. xxxi

49

tendency toward overparticularization. Master Antonio signed two large amphoras each with 1580 marked on the base, decorated with Raphaelesque motifs, formerly in the Spitzer Collection. Alfonso, who seems to have painted in another artist's workshop, signed a plate with Romulus receiving the Sabine Women, now in the Victoria and Albert Museum. Francesco was head of the workshop in the year 1608, as is proved by a three-lobed wine cooler formerly in the Fountaine Collection, with a scene of Adam and Eve in Paradise, within a border of grotesques. Certain characteristics of the Patanazzi are seen in the Raphaelesque ornament on the service with the heraldic device of Alfonso II of Este, although it is doubtful whether this can be assigned to Urbino rather than Ferrara.

Pesaro and the cities of the Adriatic coast At Pesaro, another great center in the Duchy of Urbino, where, in fact, the Court resided for some time, the ceramic tradition, apparently an ancient one, is shown at its best in a series of vessels dated 1540 to 1542 from the workshop of Gerolamo di Lanfranco dalle Gabicce. Among these are the bowl with the Creation of the Animals, dated 1540, now in the Ashmolean Museum of Oxford. Another bowl with Cicero and Julius Caesar as Legis- FIG. xxxiii lators, in the British Museum, which bears the date 1542, mentions the workshop of FIG. xxxiv *mastro gironimo da le Gabice*, and, later on, the plate with Women Bathing, now in the Museo Civico of Bologna, which has on the back the inscription *in botega di mo Gironimo vasaro, iachomo pinsur* (in the workshop of Gerolamo the potter, painted by Jacomo). This dish, painted by Gerolamo's son, like the others, has *istoriato* decoration painted all over the surface, as was common in Urbino. Although in the style of Urbino, these pieces from Pesaro strike a new note, because of their decided trend toward pictorialism, accentuated by the loosening of the forms of the designs, by their manner of shading, by the predominance of a rather brownish orange, and by the trick of marking with minute strokes the outlines of stones in mural structures. The activity of the Pesaro majolica works, which Passeri recognizes in what seems, rather, the province of the Umbrian workshops, is confirmed by examples with precise markings of locality and workshop, and by other works, dated or otherwise, that resemble them closely, as well as by documents in the archives and by the results of excavations. These last reveal also the knowledge of a variety of minor styles of ornamentation, which connect the work of Pesaro with that of neighboring and distant centers, on the coast and further inland. The privilege granted in 1569 by Guidobaldo II to Giacomo di Gerolamo Lanfranco, "who has after many experiments found the way to put real gold on vases of terracotta," might be understood in connection with some later lustered plates, which are, however, not clearly distinguishable from the art of Deruta.

A few miles to the north, still on the Adriatic coast, is Rimini which, with Ravenna and Pesaro, according to Piccolpasso, furnished the clay for the workshops of Venice. Rimini PL. 73 made no noticeable impression on the history of majolica, because of the sporadic nature of its work, and the continuous oscillations of taste between the focal zones of Faenza and Urbino, according to the origin of the artisans gathered within its walls.

In 1535 Rimini gave hospitality to Giulio da Urbino, who, in Master Alessandro's workshop, painted the large jug now in the Museo Civico of Bologna with the story of Minos and Scylla, and is perhaps the author of the fine little series of *istoriato* plates, marked with place and date, which we have already mentioned.

Faenza was the most vigorous and independent center to submit to the dominant style of Urbino, toward the middle of the century, as is shown in examples of this period from the workshops of the Manaras, of Virgiliotto Calamelli, of Francesco Risino, and the Dalle Palle family, of whom one member, Gianbattista, was in 1563 signing works in Verona. *Late masters of istoriato at Faenza, Ravenna, Forlì*

XXX

XXX INTERIOR OF "ISTORIATO" WINE COOLER FROM SERVICE FOR GUIDOBALDO II. URBINO, WORKSHOP OF ORAZIO FONTANA (1565-71). FLORENCE, BARGELLO.

xxxi

xxxii

xxxiii

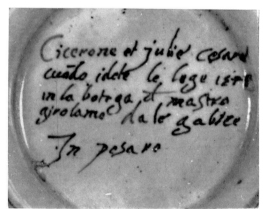

xxxiv

xxxi PLATE WITH BACCHUS AND RAPHAELESQUE DECORATION. URBINO, PATANAZZI WORKSHOP (LATE 16TH CENT.). VENICE, MUSEO CIVICO CORRER.
xxxii PANEL, SGRAFFITO OVER SLIP, WITH BUST OF ARISTOTLE IN LOW RELIEF. PADUA (EARLY 16TH CENT.). ROTTERDAM, BOYMANS-VAN BEUNINGEN MUSEUM. *xxxiii* BOWL WITH CICERO AND JULIUS CAESAR. PESARO, WORKSHOP OF GIROLAMO DALLE GABICCE (1542). LONDON, BRITISH MUSEUM. *xxxiv* INSCRIPTION ON BACK OF BOWL WITH CICERO AND JULIUS CAESAR.

The influence of the manner of Pellipario has already been pointed out in the works of Baldassare Manara. The evolution toward more complicated compositions and more varied palettes—although Faenza was always more restrained in the arrangement of colors and did not allow the richer tones to predominate—that we see in Urbino in the works of the Fontana family can be traced also in examples from those Faventine workshops which, in the wide commercial transactions that carried Faventine wares to faraway markets, reflected the prevailing fashion. The mark of Virgiliotto's workshop, one of the greatest in the city between 1531 and 1570, is found not only on molded bowls and vases, with their ornamentation divided into compartments of diverse colors, but also on vessels decorated all over in the *istoriato* style, like the great plate in the Berlin Schlossmuseum, with the Sacrifice of Marcus Curtius, and the *crespina* (small molded bowl on a foot) of the Dutuit Collection at the Petit Palais in Paris, with St. Francis receiving the Stigmata. It is seen as well on the plate, dated 1543, at the Victoria and Albert Museum, with the allegory of the Church Triumphant, and in another, in the same museum, with Alexander placing the works of Homer in the Tomb of Achilles, dated toward the end of 1575, and showing also the mark of the same workshop.

Francesco Risino, alias Mezzarisa, is another famous potter and painter of whom we hear between 1527 and 1581, when he was drawing up contracts for considerable supplies of ware to be sent to Genoa, to Naples, and even to Sicily. He also had business connections with monasteries in Ravenna and Brescia and with the Court of Ferrara. We know of some panels painted by him. Two of these portray the Crucifixion, after Raphael, one, dated 1544, is at the Palermo Museum, the other at the British Museum. A third panel with figures, dated 1546, now in an American private collection, bears on the back the inscription *Misser Giovanni Bramé di Palermo in Faenza,*

which appears to refer to the merchant from Palermo, of Ligurian origin, who introduced Risino to the Sicilian market and whom some even take to be the painter of this work.

As we have already pointed out, all the workshops of the Romagna carried on their art in the same way and presented no noticeable differences among themselves. We must mention here the workshops of Forlì, which, in some pieces signed by Eleucadio PL. 74 Solombrino, and in others dated between 1542 and 1564, with or without place indications, now in the Museums of Bologna and Ravenna, at the Louvre, and in the Victoria and Albert Museum, show the tendency to submit to the prevailing dictates of fashion. Sometimes, as in the plate at the Ravenna Museum, with Horsemen before a Triumphal Arch, the scene is framed in a wide border of polychrome grotesques on a dark-blue ground.

After Forlì we come to Ravenna. Excavations in its neighborhood have unearthed fragments, with the mark of the city, decorated in compartments or *alla porcellana*. Cesena and Imola, and all the region up to Bologna, just beyond the Romagna, were flooded with potters from Faenza who attended the weekly markets and sometimes remained to work there for varying periods. We must speak also of one place in the Romagna that belonged to the Duchy of Ferrara and was on the border of Faventine territory, that is, of Cotignola, the home of the Sforzas, less than 10 miles from Faenza—although our knowledge is limited to the names of potters discovered by research in the archives or to findings from chance excavations.

The close contact between artisans and their frequent transfer from one place to another explain Piccolpasso's references to the "Ferrarese white," of which we shall say more later, and the close resemblance to Faventine work of products that were presumably made in the Ferrarese zone.

From the Romagna we pass to the Veneto. *The Veneto* We have already mentioned the sojourn in Verona of Gianbattista Dalle Palle. Besides the plates dated 1547 and 1563, we must also mention a document of 1499 in which is recorded the testimony given in Venice by one Antonio, from Faenza, a potter of Verona. On the other hand, the Veronese territory itself, for example at Legnago, has often given proof of ceramic activity, especially in vessels of the Faventine style, covered with slip and sgraffito. Padua must be numbered among the most important centers of Faenza ware with sgraffito decoration over a slip coating and for the variety of types and the volume of production during the fifteenth and sixteenth centuries. We must add that this art was accompanied by remarkable activity also in the field of majolica. Evidence is furnished by documents in the archives and from literary sources which describe a fairly restless colony of potters from the Romagna and especially from Faenza in this cosmopolitan university city of St. Anthony. These potters, who enjoyed particular privileges, flocked there also to sell their products at the great annual fair.

At Padua, also, excavations have brought to light, together with sgraffito ware, majolica pieces ornamented with blue and white foliage on a lavender-gray enamel, or with polychrome flowers and twigs, also on a lavender-gray ground, sometimes enlivened with little blue dots, and other details from the same vocabulary of ornamentation. These pieces evidently once formed part of services belonging to the monastic orders, such as the Camaldolesi of the famous Abbazia di Carceri d'Este. An obvious imitation of Middle Eastern models is seen in some pieces, such as the so-called "Candian" ware, reserved for the services of a convent of nuns at the end of the sixteenth century and the beginning of the seventeenth. The inscription *a Padoa* is found, sometimes accompanied by a little cross, on the back of plates dated 1548 and 1564, in the Cluny Museum and the British Museum. One is decorated with a border of dark-blue woven design, the other with yellow concentric circles. On the front of these plates

the figures of Adam and Eve and of Hercules and Galatea, like other figures with the same characteristics at the Victoria and Albert and British Museums (Myrrha fleeing from her Father, dated 1548; the Sacrifice of Marcus Curtius, dated 1550; Circe, dated 1563), are inexpertly painted in brown on a thin white or grayish enamel.

In the Veneto, attention must center on the capital city, Venice, whose potters produced both sgraffito and enamel ware. Thanks to the numerous examples which Conton recovered from the Lagoon some decades ago, Venice is known to have been among the most important centers of the production of sgraffito ware in the period between the fifteenth and the eighteenth centuries. During the sixteenth century the Venetians acquired a well-deserved renown for their enamel ware. *Venice*

The fifteenth-century slip bowls have strongly drawn female, or occasionally male, busts, or symbolic animals, such as the dog and rabbit, set in flowery meadows, or the owner's coat of arms. The plates are adorned with interwoven geometric designs, or with borders of foliage, sometimes with figures enclosed within an architectural framework. These Venetian vessels, more clearly related to the models found also at Padua than are the flasks and jugs, of which we have few examples, have polychrome marbled decoration in green and tawny yellow, and a frugal use of blue and purple. The later, less elegant, models of Venetian ware, dating from the late sixteenth century and the early seventeenth, intended for practical use in the kitchen, show a whole series of inscriptions describing the functions for which they were destined, generally framed in wreaths of foliage or in tiny patterned borders. PL. 14

This similarity in the work of Venice and Padua, and of course by extension in that of Verona and Treviso, may be said to characterize the Venetian group, which is differentiated from the Emilian-Ferrarese-Bolognese group by the latter's harder, more strongly FIG. xxxii

PL. 13

defined designs, reflecting at times the art of Cossa with Gothic festoons in the backgrounds and at other times the Tuscan style, possibly of a later date, more sober in color, rarely marbleized and adorned only with a heraldic device in a garland of indented leaves, ribbons, and geometric motifs.

Venetian enameled faïence was probably inspired by motifs drawn from Ming porcelain and its Damascene interpretations toward the end of the fifteenth century and at the beginning of the sixteenth. The contacts with Faenza, which (after the death of Alexander VI and the consequent failure of Valentino's dream of carving out for himself a principality in the Romagna) gave itself up voluntarily for a few years (1504–09) to the Venetian Republic, helped to bind these two centers together also in the field of majolica. The Faventine potters obtained from the Republic special concessions for their participation in markets and fairs in Venetian territory, concessions which were codified in a document used throughout the sixteenth century. In both places the artists increased and diffused the adoption of the "porcelain" and arabesque styles of ornamentation, and of the decoration in blue and white upon lavender-gray enamel. The former style is shown in some plates, with the arms of German families, attributed to the period 1520–30, now in the Museums of Berlin and Frankfurt, plates in which the leafy sprays and the clearly distinguishable lotus flowers faithfully preserve the appearance of the original porcelain, whereas in the potteries of Faenza the round flower, identified as the chrysanthemum, is more and more frequently seen among the sprays. The decoration on lavender-gray enamel was much used later on, between 1540 and 1550, by the decorators of the workshops of Master Lodovico, in the quarter of S. Paolo, and in those of Master Jacopo da Pesaro, in the quarter of S. Barnaba.

From the workshop of Master Lodovico came a plate, now in the Victoria and Albert Museum, ornamented with *cerquate*, that is,

a motif of interwoven branches and leaves of the oak tree, enclosing a central trophy. On the back, under a shield with a cross, is the inscription *In Venetia, in co[n]trada di S.to Polo in botega di M. Lodovico* (In Venice, in Master Lodovico's shop in St. Paul's quarter). A similar design is shown on another plate, with a rim bordered with foliage, fruit, and birds and a mermaid in the center. It bears on the back the inscription *1540. Adì 16 del mexe de oturbe* (1540. The 16th of the month of October). This plate, now in the Ashmolean Museum in Oxford, may be assigned to the same workshop. Both these plates and others of a later date, adorned with leaves, gadroons, and landscapes with or without scenes with figures, and sometimes inspired by the compositions of master engravers, are painted in blue and white on colored enamel; on the back is usually a "porcelain" spray pattern, sketchily drawn.

FIG. XXXV

The same fashion, painting in blue and white on gray enamel, is shown in work from the shop of Master Jacopo da Pesaro, whose name appears on plates and bowls now in the Wallace Collection, in the Victoria and Albert Museum, and also in the Sigmaringen Museum, dated 1542 and 1543. Here we see also the "basket" openwork form of the bowl, and in the decoration a particular fondness for busts, sometimes framed in arabesques or candelabra.

There was a third workshop, with a larger repertory of designs, that flourished some years later and was therefore more sensitive to the influence of Faenza and Urbino. We find its indications upon plates and drugpots at the Herzog Anton Ulrich Museum of Brunswick, the Kunstgewerbemuseum of Frankfurt-am-Main, and the Berlin Schlossmuseum, as well as in private collections. The fullest inscription is upon a plate at Brunswick, with Moses and Aaron before Pharaoh: *1568 Zener Domenigo da Venecia feci in la botega al ponteselo p[er] andar a san polo* (1568, Zener Domenico from Venice made it in the workshop near the bridge

53

leading to S. Paolo). This makes it clear that other plates and vases must belong to this workshop, whether or not they have the inscription *Domenigo da Venecia* or the date 1568, provided they are ornamented with "stories" or with strongly drawn polychrome busts, which already show the increasing influence of the *compendiario* style (a manner of painting in short strokes) and the attempt to represent form with color rather than with line. The latter is a reflection of the manner of the great masters of sixteenth-century Venetian painting, which gives these wares a quality of softness and fluidity not known in their prototypes in Urbino. The scenes and the busts are framed in riotous garlands of leaves, fruit, and flowers, painted in the most lively colors on a deep dark-blue ground, which is in its turn adorned with sgraffito arabesques that expose the white of the enamel.

FIG. XXXVI

To the workshop "near the stonecutter's bridge leading to S. Paolo," as it is more precisely indicated on a large plate in the Cora Collection in Florence, must be attributed also some vessels painted in blue and white on a lavender-gray enamel. To this series belongs a large plate in the Vatican Museum, with a Peasant Girl standing spinning by the chimney, in a rim bordered with fruit and flowers, painted with a breadth of stroke that reminds us of other dishes, also decorated in polychrome upon lavender-gray enamel, at the Victoria and Albert Museum and the Museum of Faenza. Other plates with warlike trophies and figures relate the output of Master Domenico's workshop to that of the workshops of Master Lodovico and Master Giacomo. To these, but showing a more marked leaning toward the style of Urbino, may be added the workshop of Guido di Merlino (or Merligo), who seems to have been working in Venice in 1542.

PL. 75

Not long after the middle of the sixteenth century, as is generally agreed to be proved by documents in the archives and by dated examples, we notice the appearance in Faenza, and the rapid and successful diffusion in other centers in the South and North and even beyond the Alps, of a new kind of ware called "white ware," which was to outlive the sixteenth century and persist, still full of vitality, until the end of the seventeenth.

Piccolpasso who, as we have already said, wrote his "Three books on the potter's art" about the year 1556 or 1557, repeatedly refers to this ware, although he calls it *bianco del Duca di Ferrara, malamente detto bianco faentino* (white ware of the Duke of Ferrara, wrongly called "white ware of Faenza"). His remarks prove, however, that even at its first appearance, the Faenza workshops which produced the white ware were very widely known. Piccolpasso is contradicted by Cellini, who, in that part of his memoirs in which he tells of his brief sojourn in Ferrara in 1540, speaks of a "jug of white terracotta of that Faventine terracotta, very delicately wrought." Another refutation is provided by documents in the archives which affirm that Master Francesco Mezzarisa of Faenza, abovementioned, had already, since February, 1540, taken into his employment on a five-year contract a Master Pietro, "son of the late Master Francesco Zambalini," for the particular and exclusive task of *concordare totum colorem album* (producing totally white ware).

The white ware must have been appearing in ever greater quantities in the ware supplied by Mezzarisa, but if we remember that Faenza is only a few miles away from the Duchy of Ferrara and that exchanges of craftsmen have been amply proved from documents, we can easily understand the writer's confusion. In any case, in the third book, Piccolpasso, after saying that "for the Ferrarese white ware the glaze is made of double the usual thickness," continues: "upon this they paint with black and blue cobalt, that is, with the black they draw the outlines and with the blue they do the shading, and they paint them with deep orange and pale yellow, and with nothing else, taking care to put the colors on clean."

54

xxxv

xxxvi

xxxvii

XXXV PLATE WITH "BERETTINO" BLUE-GRAY ENAMEL, WITH MERMAID, AND BRIM WITH FOLIAGE DECORATION. VENICE, WORKSHOP OF MASTER LODOVICO (1540). OXFORD, ASHMOLEAN MUSEUM. *XXXVI* JUG WITH FIGURE. GROUND DECORATED WITH LEAVES, FLOWERS, AND FRUIT. POLYCHROME ON DARK BLUE. VENICE, WORKSHOP OF MASTER DOMENICO (CA. 1560). VENICE, MUSEO CIVICO CORRER. *XXXVII* BALUSTER VASES WITH HANDLES IN SHAPE OF SPHINXES. FAENZA (EARLY 17TH CENT.). FAENZA MUSEUM.

xxxviii

xxxix

xl

xli

xxxviii TWO-HANDLED VASE WITH ALLEGORY OF FORTUNE. APULIA (17TH CENT.). LONDON, VICTORIA AND ALBERT MUSEUM. *xxxix* PLATE WITH HUNTING SCENE. CASTELLI, STYLE OF ANTONIO LOLLI (FIRST HALF OF 17TH CENT.). FAENZA MUSEUM. *xl* PHARMACY VASE. TRAPANI (1698). FAENZA MUSEUM. *xli* PAVEMENT TILES WITH BIRDS. CALTAGIRONE (16TH CENT.). CALTAGIRONE, COLL. IN MUSEO DELL'ISTITUTO D'ARTE.

Piccolpasso, who had been in the workshop of Virgiliotto at Faenza, where he had seen a fine red, here points with masterly precision to the essential quality of white ware: thick over-all enamel glaze and a palette limited to dark and pale blue, yellow, and orange. After the pictorial deviations to which the *istoriato* had gradually led during the course of the century, the new style returned to the essential values which had been to some extent forgotten: line, form, plastic aspect, volume. Here lay the secret of its success. The sobriety of color, in strong contrast to the palette habitually saturated with colors and their complements, was allied to the *compendiario* style, which, unlike the classical *istoriato*, maintained the lively fancy and the freshness and immediacy of invention of a rapid sketch. Another quality that contributed to its extraordinary popularity was the soft, velvety, pure surface of the enamel, left largely unadorned, the better to show it off. Not only did these white pieces soon take their place alongside the everyday ware and the ware without figure ornamentation which is common to the repertory of every pottery, but sometimes, by virtue of their prodigious vitality, superseded all other types.

Factors that helped to introduce the new style and to make it popular were the sense of staleness aroused by half a century of overworked polychrome *istoriato*, the fondness for new molded forms resulting from the popularity of the silver and bronze ware that had partly taken the place of pewter and seemed inspired by the taste for Mannerism and the incipient Baroque, and the need to set off these molded forms with an enamel not reduced to the function of a mere background for pictorial decoration, however attractive that might be. Table services, *credenze*—now composed of numerous pieces—with plates, dishes, egg-stands, saltcellars, fruit dishes, ewers, wine coolers, candelabra, and "triumphal groups" are now made of smooth white majolica. Besides these table services the potters made drugpots, flasks, phials for pharmacies, inkstands, lamps, groups of figures, busts, obelisks, and pavement tiles.

The decoration less and less followed the *istoriato* fashion, covering entire surfaces with Biblical, historical, and mythological scenes and religious images, rapidly sketched in the *compendiario* manner, in a restrained blue-yellow-orange color combination, or decorated with Raphaelesque fantasies. More frequently, however, it was limited to the figure of a winged *amorino* holding a disk or an arrow, or of a woman, a knight, a saint, or the design of a coat of arms, sometimes within a border formed by a slender spray with leaves and tendrils encircling the edge of the rim, or by circular bands of decorative motifs derived from embroidery, painted in dark-blue monochrome.

PL. 76

The workshop of Francesco Mezzarisa, in which in 1556 Antonio Romanino Cimatti painted figured scenes on the large drugpot now at the Faenza Museum, welcomed the new models. Virgiliotto Calamelli's workshop, in fact, replaced the traditional *istoriato* ornamentation, with its borders divided into compartments, with *crespine* (molded dishes with a foot) and white services like those for Monsignor Alberico de Alberici di Bologna and for Don Aloisio d'Este, of which we read in an inventory of the same year, 1556. These dishes are marked with the initials of the shop: VR AF.

The workshop of Leonardo Battisi, who was called Don Pino and signed his work "Do Pi," supplied a rich service for the Bavarian Royal House, now preserved in Munich and left records in the archives of large orders supplied to the municipality, by the donation of persons of high rank. There were also the shops of Domenico Pirotti and, later on, of Vicchi, the Mazzanti, and many others who produced ware in the same style.

The great demand for white ware and the abundant productivity of the workshops resulted in the distribution of this ware all over Italy and beyond the Alps. In France the name of the city of its origin became famous: Faenza became faïence. In the same way in which Arras had given its name to tapestries and Damascus to a cloth, so faïence indicated the ware, white or otherwise, that originated in Faenza and afterward was produced also in other places, near and far. What happened in France also occurred in many other European countries.

To this diffusion of works we must add the dispersal of craftsmen. In Turin, Genoa, Verona, Padua, Deruta, Castelli d'Abruzzo, in Apulia, and abroad in Lyons and Le Croisic in France, and in Holland and England also were to be found the products and the masters of the *compendiario*, enticed far from their own land by the offer of more favorable conditions for work, or driven by the desire for wealth, or sometimes by political and religious necessities.

It is almost certainly due to religious persecution that we find Swiss, German, Bohemian, Hungarian, and Moravian examples of majolica. The contacts which, through their work, the Faventine masters maintained with the Reformation countries had facilitated the introduction of heresy within their own walls. The infection of heresy spread widely in every class, and provoked the fierce intervention of the Inquisition Tribunals, which succeeded in extirpating it by using every kind of weapon, including the gallows, imprisonment, and burning at the stake. Faenza had its own martyrs. Theodorus Beza himself, Calvin's successor at Geneva, had words of praise for Fanino Fanini, executed at Faenza in August, 1550; many others, however, found a refuge among their own coreligionists. This flight of artisans was responsible for the appearance, among the ceramic wares produced and used by the *habani* heretical communities in Central Europe, at the end of the sixteenth century and throughout the seventeenth, forms and ornamentation obviously inspired by models from the Faventine workshops. These forms were maintained, with more or less noticeable variations, in the ceramic repertory of these communities, even after their reabsorption in the great Catholic family.

Emigration was not, however, limited to craftsmen responsible for white ware and *compendiario* ornamentation. It is true that at the important cultural and commercial center of Lyons, Henry III in 1574 granted letters patent with privileges to Domenico Tardessir and Giuliano Gambini of Faenza. At Nantes in 1580 Jean Ferro di Altare opened a factory for white ware, possibly one of the enterprises encouraged by royal patronage in this field. In 1554, however, Gian Francesco Pesaro had already been granted the same patents and privileges. From 1506 on, as we have said, there were certainly Italian artisans in Lyons. It was at the instance of Cardinal De Tournon, Archbishop of the city since 1551, that Piccolpasso wrote his treatise on the potter's art, by means of which the prelate may have intended to impart valuable information to the artisans of the city.

From 1494 to 1502 a Girolamo Solombrino from Forlì was at Amboise; in 1509 the Ridolfi brothers from Cafaggiolo had a factory at Machetone in Brittany; François I summoned Girolamo di Andrea della Robbia to his court to build for him in the Bois de Boulogne the Château de Madrid, the *château de faïence*, as Philibert Delorme called it; between 1566 and 1585 the Conrades of Albisola established themselves at Nevers.

It was through the instruction received from the Italian artisans, and also through the patronage of the Constable Anne de Montmorency, a great lover of Italian majolica, that the French were able, in the sixteenth century, to set up their own famous potteries directed by French artists, which produced superb pavements with Raphaelesque decoration, like those from the workshop of Masseot Abaquesne at Rouen, and plates and flasks of obvious Faventine inspiration, like those produced by Antoine Siyalon at Nîmes.

In the Low Countries, Guido di Savino of Casteldurante, alias Guido Andries, was already established at Antwerp in 1510, and there trained his sons who afterward spread the art to Holland and to England. A Venetian, Pier

56

Francesco, in 1532 executed a pavement in the Abbey of Herckenrode, near Hasselt, with arabesques and Persian palmettes forming a border for busts and portraits. Local artisans, such as Jan Van den Bogaert, trained by the Italians, emigrated from Antwerp to Portugal, and to Holland and Germany.

At first the Dutch production, which in the late sixteenth century came from the hands of potters from the southern part of the Low Countries, reflected Italian models in its geometric schemes and its polychrome flowers and fruit. In the white ware it imitated the forms, the enamel, and the designs of the *compendiario*, and its Raphaelesque decoration so resembled the Urbinate prototypes that it was described as the Patanazzi of Delft type. On the other hand, artisans from Haarlem were also responsible for introducing the art into Delft, and a painter-potter from Haarlem, Hendrik Cornelisz Vroom, born in 1566, visited the potteries of many European cities, including Seville, Florence, Rome, Venice, Milan, Genoa, Albisola, and Lyons, before returning to his own land, where he died in 1640. In North Germany a Johannes Guldens, a resident of Antwerp, who had lived for many years in Italy, in the closing years of the century applied to the magistrature of Hamburg for the privilege of setting up a factory of majolica *italico more* (in the Italian style). In the South, in Bavaria, the scions of noble families or of rich merchants, while studying in Italy, encouraged the taste for Italian art by firsthand commissioning of table vessels, plates, and services with heraldic arms, as we have already mentioned.

In Carniola, in Austria, in the year 1534, Ferdinand I granted privileges to a Pietro Reicher of Lubiana for the manufacture of bowls, jugs, and other painted vases "as are made in Venice."

In Poland, where pavements in the Italian style are still being discovered in the old castles, Antonio Destesi, an Italian resident at Cracow who enjoyed privileges granted by King Stephen Batory, summoned two artists from Faenza, Michele Tonducci and Clemente Avezzuti, in an unsuccessful attempt to introduce the art into that city in the years 1584 and 1585. At Corfu, according to Piccolpasso, the Gatti brothers from Casteldurante worked for some time.

Before the general adoption of the fashion for dark-blue monochrome, caused by the large-scale importation of Chinese porcelains through the agency of the various companies of the Indies, and particularly through that of the Dutch Company, and by the imitations of those exotic products produced in Delft and in other Netherlandish centers, the color and inventive fancy of the Italian art had attracted producers and patrons from every part of Europe.

At the end of the sixteenth and the beginning of the seventeenth century, fifty years after its invention, white ware still had an intense vitality which encouraged its diffusion and its development throughout the seventeenth century.

On the one hand, pictorialism and the love of over-all painted surfaces—a kind of horror vacui (which, one must note, never entirely disappeared from the practice of the workshops)—led to a return to the painting of religious images and scenes, or complicated mythological subjects, upon dishes or mural panels of varying size, as we see in some examples from the workshop and the brush of those cousins of the same name, Battista Mazzanti, who worked in Faenza during the first half of the century, and in later examples painted by Francesco Cavina in the workshop of Francesco Vicchi.

We find also, owing partly to the attraction felt for exotic schemes of ornamentation, designs of flowery sprays adorned with animals and insects, which now cover the entire surface of drugpots, flasks, ewers, amphoras, and even of plates, usurping the space formerly reserved for Raphaelesque decoration. In both these styles we see the constant trend toward the *compendiario* manner, even when the

PL. 77

FIGS. *i*, xxxvii

painter's palette is enriched with a new color, yellowish or pea green (obtained by mixing yellow and blue), and, later on, by the introduction of manganese purple for outlines.

On the other hand, especially in the widely diffused and much-prized table services, in "show dishes," and above all, in molded ware, the tendency is now to exclude all trace of ornament or to restrict it, at most, to a heraldic device or to the owner's initials. In the potteries of Faenza the color scheme is kept within the colors of the *compendiario* palette: dark blue and orange-yellow, with the occasional addition of a threadlike manganese brown.

It is indeed in the white ware that the daring spirit of Baroque virtuosity finds expression in the ceramic field. It is found in smooth flat dishes of unusual size, and in molded forms inspired by originals wrought in gold, silver, bronze, or copper, which have complicated shapes, internal divisions, gadroons, and bosses, with applied plastic monsters, such as sphinxes, harpies, mermaids, and serpents twisted to make handles, cartouches, bands, and other applied elements. It is also found in designs that imitate the art of weaving or braiding, in the openwork *crespine* or PL. 78 the hanging lamps, cages, obelisks, and other fantastic objects, which no longer show any restraint or any respect for the particular qualities of the material used.

This daring and these innovations found, especially in Northern Europe and in the northern Low Countries, admirers and imitators who produced not only flower vases in the shape of pyramids or arches or open hands but also shoes, slippers, hammers, and violins! They were, naturally, not copied to such an extent, or in the same manner, in those centers—and there were many on both sides of the Alps—which had welcomed the style of the white ware. In the same way, the *compendiario* itself was not understood and expressed in the same way in every place, nor was it always restricted to the typical color range. Certainly it was the *compendiario*, in

spite of the occasional excesses provoked by the *virtuosi* and by Baroque taste, which restored to the art of *faïence* a decorative sense more consonant with its own capabilities.

In the first half of the eighteenth century these two tendencies, toward plain white surfaces or toward scenes with polychrome or monochrome figures, were reflected in Faenza in large dishes of varying sizes, smooth or molded, in jugs and other receptacles. The white ware was adorned, at most, with a narrow border of a corbel-like design, in blue or in yellow and orange, encircling the outer edge. The painted scenes included pastoral and religious subjects by an anonymous painter who worked for the Ferniani factory, and perhaps for that other which was at one time, between 1740 and 1757, directed by Antonio Maria Regoli.

In Central and Southern Italy, as well as in the North, the *compendiario* presented noticeable modifications. It was certainly introduced into Deruta, during the sixteenth century, by potters from Faenza, of whom we have documentary evidence. This is proved also by the close resemblance in form and in the composition of the enamel of the *crespine* and the large dishes produced by these shops, as well as by the style of ornamentation. Distinguishing features may be pointed out, such as the rigidity of the trailing sprays bordering the rims and the almost regular addition of green in the brief sketches of landscape against which the *putti* and other figures are set, treated in a mature impressionistic spirit.

This coloristic deviation was to be intensified in the course of the seventeenth century, also because of the attraction felt for the Raphaelesque designs of the traditional Urbinate style, and perhaps for the lively polychrome of the works which, with ever-increasing success, issued from the Tuscan potteries of Montelupo.

A very characteristic production of the Deruta potteries in the seventeenth century was connected with the cult of the miraculous

Influence of white ware at Deruta

58

image known as the *Madonna dei Bagni*, preserved in a sanctuary in the parish of Casilina near Deruta. The image, a bust of the Virgin with the Child in her arms, is often found painted on goblets and plates, traced somewhat sketchily in manganese brown with shading of reddish orange, sometimes framed in a Raphaelesque border. It is also reproduced on a rich series of votive tablets with polychrome figures, painted more or less expertly, which, although they express sentiments of piety and gratitude, are unconsciously related to the typical moralizing narrative style of Deruta works of the early and late sixteenth century, and contain formal imitations of these masters.

FIG. *xlii*

In Latium, Rome cannot be said to have had any particular style of her own. Rome was a cosmopolitan center sensitive to the Umbrian influence, and the influx of artists and products from other regions, especially from the Romagna, the Marches, Tuscany, and Liguria, created a variety of types without unifying characteristics, apart from the attenuated vigor of the particular regional styles.

Influence of compendiario at Montelupo

In Tuscany, Montelupo achieved well-deserved renown in the late sixteenth century and the early seventeenth when the potteries of Florence and Cafaggiolo were no longer famous. These centers also had maintained a lofty tradition, as Guasti's research in the archives proves, at least from the second half of the fourteenth century. The consistency of the ceramic art of the sixteenth century is attested by the Statutes of the Potters' "University," which thirty-four directors and masters of the art drew up, when revising and amplifying previous conventions in 1510, "considering how useful to the Citadel is the art of the potters and vase makers, so that almost all the population is fed by their industry, and considering also how burdened and oppressed are the poor craftsmen, because of the difficulty of procuring from the merchants and agents the materials necessary for this work, that is, cobalt, tin, lead, etc."

xlii VOTIVE PANEL. DERUTA (1662). DERUTA, SANCTUARY OF MADONNA DEI BAGNI.

Our imperfect knowledge of the marks and the difficulty of deciphering those which distinguish pieces generally attributed to Florentine and other Tuscan potteries, like those of Cafaggiolo, do not permit us to ascribe many works with any certainty to the potters of Montelupo. Chance excavations in that locality, however, attest to the variety of their repertory and their color range, both of which are based on a thematic development clearly "severe" in character. The sixteenth century saw polychrome motifs used as well as the blue monochrome inspired by China, which is here rendered with sprays and foliage that have lost much of their exotic character, as a border for landscapes and birds painted in the wells of the plates, and a green foliage motif scattered all over the surface. Potters from Montelupo also worked in many places outside Tuscany, while potters from other centers were present at Montelupo. In fact, in the second half of the century Guasti finds the names of some artists from Faenza. Perhaps it was they who introduced the *compendiario*, which revolutionized taste in PL. 80 these workshops too, as seems evident from the style of certain jugs with lively female heads enclosed within the characteristic broad, round rim, divided into radiating sections.

These are preserved in the Museum of Faenza.

It must be pointed out that the *compendiario* is restricted here to the pictorial manner, as these masters do not seem either to have adopted the dense, hard, brilliant enamel on the broad white surfaces which served to display it or to have reduced their palette to blue, yellow, and orange. The *compendiario* in Montelupo presents a bold, free, sketchy pictorial style, soldiers, halberdiers, *Gonfalonieri*, with robes painted in checks or stripes, heads with flowing moustaches, heroic figures, PLS. 81, 82 curvetting horses with roundly drawn haunches, all are painted in dark blue, manganese brown, green, and orange, often upon a yellow ground, and all over the surface of the plate. The mocking burlesque spirit of these scenes is frequently continued in the witty inscriptions that adorn the jugs, many of which, according to Botti who wrote at the beginning of the nineteenth century, were collected by a friar, Padre Carlo da Saragossa, at the beginning of the seventeenth century, and later destroyed by his successors.

At the climax of their development, in the first half of the seventeenth century, Cosimo II asked the potteries of Montelupo to supply the pavements which, in 1611 and 1614, he sent as a present to his cousin Marie de Médicis, Queen of France, the wife, and later the widow, of Henry IV. Examples dated 1627, 1632, and 1639 (this last with the signature *Raffaello Girolamo fecit Mte. Lupo*) are preserved at the Victoria and Albert Museum. In the second half of the century the potteries, although already in decline, were still producing a considerable quantity of ware. A dinner service of one hundred pieces, the dishes and goblets adorned with heraldic arms, is mentioned in a document in the State Archives of Florence, with the date December 19, 1669. A gadrooned plate with the Medici arms and the Florentine lily, painted alternately in the gadroons, now at the Victoria and Albert Museum, bears the inscription *Adi 16 di aprile Diacinto Monti di Montelupo*.

In Apulia the *compendiario* style was adopted in the composition of the enamel and in the palette used by the potters of Laterza and Grottaglie (called *stangatari*, *piattari*, or *faenzari*) and of numerous other centers, such as Martinafranca, Francavilla, Mesagne, and Nardò, but its spirit does not seem to have been understood there, for the design seems calligraphic, outlined academically. It is also submerged in the decorative exuberance of the Byzantine tradition, which was renewed by trade relations with the Turkish Middle East at Constantinople, with Albania and Slavonia, and also by the contribution of Spain to which Apulia, in the seventeenth century, was dynastically attached.

To the same kingdom belonged Naples and Campania which, throughout the seventeenth century, offered what is perhaps the most sumptuous expression of the use of majolica in architecture, in the rich, ornate polychrome pavements with foliage and flowers, scrolls, and architectural moldings, overflowing with Baroque fantasy. Cerreto, meanwhile, developed a more restrained ceramic expression.

The third of these Neapolitan regions is the Abruzzo. Here the production of majolica ware seems to have been concentrated in Castelli, in the "Sicilian Vale" below the Gran Sasso, although from time to time there may have been limited productivity in other centers also.

In the tiles with richly colored busts and heraldic arms, which seem to predate 1526, now in the pavement around and behind the altar of the little church of S. Donato at Castelli (but probably once part of the ceiling) and in some large mural tablets of a later date, there is evidence of an industry employing the forms and colors of the Faventine school of the late fifteenth and the early sixteenth century. These tiles and tablets may perhaps be attributed to members of the Pompei family, and in particular to Orazio, who left his mark on the tile with the figure of the Virgin, dated 1551. This attribution is

Influence of white ware in Apulia; in Campania

FIG. XXXVIII

Castelli d'Abruzzo

xliii DETAIL OF CEILING OF CHURCH OF S. DONATO AT CASTELLI. CASTELLI, TITO POMPEI AND OTHERS (1615-17).

confirmed by the fragments of pavement, dated 1576, composed of small hexagons decorated in threadlike white on an intensely blue enamel, arranged around little squares with rosettes painted in white, yellow, and green, in the Church of S. Maria della Spina at Isola del Gran Sasso. At Castelli a more ambitious form of expression, which was to lead to further developments, was also sought in the *compendiario* style, which was, naturally, dissimilar to the Faventine *compendiario*. Here again it was the complementary features which were most in evidence, the taste for white surfaces, the achievement of a fine enamel glaze, the abandonment of lively colors, the fondness for the sober palette of dull blue, yellow, orange, and pea green, outlined in dark blue or manganese brown are typical of this *compendiario* manner. It presents forms not always in harmony with the impressionistic spirit of the original, as we have already noticed in Apulia, and as may be seen very generally in productions of these outlying centers, especially when there were no masters from Faenza present in person.

The pea green, obtained by the mixture or superimposition of yellow and blue, is seen in some of the most characteristic works of the *compendiario* style in Castelli, for exam-

ple, in the twenty-nine superb tiles of the altar of S. Michele in the parish church. The images of saints are painted on these titles with such sincerity and power that they would have done honor to any Faventine master of the early seventeenth century, and tasteful precedents in Faenza itself can be found.

Evidence of the *compendiario* style in Castelli is found in the great pharmacy jars adorned with sprays with tendrils and flowers, painted with unusual freshness and fidelity to the models, as well as on the vases and *crespine*, which repeat in the openwork design the taste and the shapes of the Faventine white ware. The design, with its clear outline and slight shading, is in the subdued palette already described.

The most notable monument to these fashions is the ceiling of the little church of S. Donato, formed of wide tiles decorated with figured scenes, images of saints, busts, emblems, heraldic arms, foliage, and inscriptions, among which occurs the frequent repetition of the name of a certain Tito Pompei, who seems to have been one of the artists, and of the dates 1615, 1616, and 1617. The same palette and the same spirit are seen in the four panels with the Saints John the Baptist, An-

FIG. *xliii*

thony the Abbot, Apollonia, and Lucia, formerly part of a polyptic contemporary with this ceiling, from the Church of Colledoro, now preserved in the Civic Museum of Castelli.

The *compendiario* now became vulgarized in minor works to suit the popular taste, in images of saints painted on vases, pots, and small panels with which the name of Berardino Gentile il Vecchio (d. 1683) is associated. Nevertheless, it made its contribution to the formation of the particular school associated with Castelli.

The *istoriato* most used in the Marches is best seen in the works of Francesco Grue (1618–73), the head of his family. The plate marked by him in the Acerbo Collection of Loreto Aprutino, with a Meeting of Cyrus and Alexander, in fact shows an arrangement of figures in the Urbino style, rendered in unusual colors, dominated by passages shading from azure to violet, while both arrangement and color are in contrast with the prevailing manner and tonality inspired by the *compendiario*. Grue maintained this color scheme, albeit with a certain inexplicable harshness, in the 1637 panel with the Trinity, in the Civic Museum of Castelli, attributed to him, and in the altarpiece signed and dated 1607, with the Madonna of Loreto and Saints, in the parish church. In this altarpiece Grue combined azure-violet gradations with pea green, and outlined boldly in brown, perhaps in imitation of late examples of Urbino ware decorated with grotesques, thus laying the foundation of what was to become the characteristic palette of Castelli.

Grue's manner and the style of the Marches, showing a decided fondness for the pale yellows and harmonizing colors originating in the *compendiario*, may be seen in plates with FIG. xxxix battle scenes, war councils, hunting scenes, and so on, bordered with rims divided into compartments with military trophies, or with a trailing coil of leaves with *putti*. Some of these plates are earlier than Grue's own works and they lead up to the wine cooler of the

Acerbo Collection, showing episodes of the Story of David, with its delicate and discreet gilding, and to the superb round dish with foot, showing the Judgment of Paris, in the S. Martino Museum at Naples, which has the FIG. xliv inscription *Antonius Lollus a Castelli inventor*.

In the second half of the seventeenth century, as G. C. Polidori has explained, Francesco's son, Carlantonio Grue (1655–1723), introduced into majolica ware the pictorial style he had absorbed from the fresco and panel painting of the great Baroque masters, with a consequent softening of tone, a richness of color, and a sincere fondness for portraying the wooded scenery of his own countryside. This changed the art of Castelli and set it upon a plane where it was to find full scope for its development throughout the following century in the work of the descendants of his family and in that of members of the other celebrated family of majolica artists of Castelli, the Gentile.

The fondness for superimposed, or compound, colors, such as orange on yellow, pea green, gray-blue, is allied, in Carlantonio Grue, to the skillful use of manganese brown for shading, and to more robust color tones. A frugal use of gilding often enriches the palette; the landscape and the figures of children or of buxom women are enclosed within a framework in which architectural elements often appear. Among his most striking works, a considerable number of which are in the S. Martino Museum in Naples, the vase with the Flight into Egypt, after a composition by FIG. xlv Federico Barocci, in the Museo della Floridiana of the same city, must certainly be mentioned.

During the seventeenth century and at the beginning of the eighteenth, Carmine Gentile (1678–1763) and Nicola and Candeloro Cappelletti continued to work along the lines laid down by Carlantonio Grue.

In Sicily, still part of the Neapolitan kingdom, the best-known period and that of greatest expansion is to be found at the end of the sixteenth century and during the course

xliv LARGE DISH WITH JUDGEMENT OF PARIS. CASTELLI, ANTONIO LOLLI (17TH CENT.). NAPLES, MUSEO NAZIONALE DI S. MARTINO.

Sicily :
Palermo,
Trapani,
Caltagirone,
and minor
centers

of the seventeenth, although the island still derived the characteristics of its art from the Arab-Norman epoch. When more light has been thrown on this art by a more thorough study of the findings from excavations and from the archives, Sicily may, together with Apulia, aspire to a higher place in the long history of Italian majolica. The activity of its majolica artists was given a new impetus by the Renaissance, and was influenced by large-scale importations from the Continent, from Tuscany, the Romagna, the Marches, and the Veneto, whence came models that seem to have been closely copied.

Trapani and Caltagirone, the former with a more constant and closer adherence to the manner of the mainland *stile severo* and the latter, without the distractions of maritime contacts, more independent of this and to a greater extent bound to traditional Oriental and Spanish forms (not to speak of Agrigentum and Syracuse), were dominated toward the close of the sixteenth century by Palermo and by the potteries under its influence, Sciacca, Burgio, and Collesano.

The most successful period of the art of Palermo was between the end of the sixteenth century and the second decade of the seventeenth, although the dated examples belong to the years between 1599 and 1673. The designs of Faventine majolica, which was introduced into Palermo at the time of Giovanni Bramé's journey to Faenza in 1546, through the large importation of pottery he commissioned from Francesco Mezzarisa, together with the designs of the Marches, brought polychrome into favor. In Gerolamo Lazzaro's important workshop warlike trophies, incorporating the emblematic eagle, serpent, and dog, constituted the basis of the ornamentation; in the workshop of Andrea Pantaleo, who worked in the second decade of the seventeenth century, the decoration in compartments was predominant. Both trophies and compartments were accompanied by the characteristic braided or woven design, by the trailing vine on a brick-red ground,

PL. 83

and by the wreath of Della Robbian foliage, which was replaced, at the beginning of the seventeenth century, by a border of two gadroons. A Master Filippo Passalacqua and a Diego di Leo belong to the period of the decadence of Palermo majolica.

Between 1612 and 1615 Pantaleo's workshop seems to have been transferred to Sciacca, a center of majolica tradition since the fifteenth century, as is proven by documents in the archives. To the sixteenth century belong some panels, such as the one with the image of S. Calogero in the grotto of Monte Cronio, with the date 1545 and the name of the artist priest, Francesco di Xuto. Others, of later date, belong to the end of the century. Among these is the panel in the Church of the Madonna degli Infermi, with St. Anthony and the name of the artist, Salvatore di Facio. To the beginning of the seventeenth century, to 1608 and 1629, belong one panel at Caltabellotta and another at Sciacca, both decorated with images of the Madonna and Saints.

A remarkable monument is still to be seen in what is left of the large frieze formerly in the Chapel of St. George of the Genoese, 4.1 feet wide and more than 23 feet long. The frieze has been mutilated and is now composed of about three hundred tiles ($6\,5/8 \times 7$ inches) in which are represented, as if in a tapestry, medallions enclosed by floral decoration, strapwork, and candelabra, with scenes from the Old and New Testaments to illustrate the Commandments of God. Besides these "stories" the frieze once bore the effigy of the artist, Master Joseppi Maxarato, who was born in 1561 and probably died in 1624 or 1625.

Pantaleo took the designs of Palermo to Sciacca where they developed special characteristics, such as the serrated strap and the sigma, used instead of a trailing vine, and subdued colors. It is difficult to distinguish the seventeenth-century Sciacca pottery from that of Palermo.

A contemporary of Pantaleo, Master Filippo La Caxa, who was working at Sciacca about

64

xlv VASE WITH FLIGHT INTO EGYPT. CASTELLI, CARLO ANTONIO GRUE (SECOND HALF OF 17TH CENT.). NAPLES, MUSEO NAZIONALE DUCA DI MARTINA ALLA FLORIDIANA.

1612 and belonged to the same family as a Nicolò Lo Cascio who worked at Burgio during the second half of the century, brought to that town, a short distance from Sciacca, the styles of both Sciacca and Palermo, rather crudely expressed. Characteristic of Burgio, and dating between 1625 and 1703, are the trophies, with typical full-moon face, strings of little circles above and below, and the braid motif with brown centers.

The influence of Palermo was felt also at Collesano, a pottery of less importance, in which, in the late seventeenth century and the beginning of the eighteenth, the rather stale manner of its shops was revitalized, more successfully than at Burgio, by the Masters Giovanni Saldo da Polizzi and Filippo Rizzuto.

We have already referred to the noble tradition of Trapani and the importance attached, during the whole sixteenth century, to its rich and varied wares, with decorative motifs in the *stile severo*, such as scrolled foliage, the peacock feather, the Persian palmette, strapwork, leaves in the Gothic-floral style, busts with characteristic profiles, and so on. These all together form a subject still too little explored for us to be able to determine the Sicilian contribution to the national art of majolica. The name of one master, Nicola Luxutusu, which appears on a drugpot with scrolled foliage, recalls the artist of the panel with S. Calogero at Sciacca. In the seventeenth century there were also produced at Trapani drugpots and large jars with me-

FIG. *xl*

dallions framed in green leaves, enclosing heraldic arms and busts, with the other side adorned with foliage sketched in a manner reminiscent of the "porcelain" motif, or decorated with geometric patterns. Both these ornamental schemes are painted in a clear blue, which verges on violet. Examples dated, and others signed, reveal the name of a Vincenzo Giacalone who was working there in the years 1674 and 1678.

We have also referred to the ancient tradition of Caltagirone in Eastern Sicily. Devastated by earthquakes, disastrous also for the documentation of ceramics, this center had enjoyed the title of the Sicilian Faenza, because of the wealth of literary evidence, the findings from archives and excavations, and the uninterrupted activity of its potteries. Caltagirone, at least in the later centuries, does not seem to have cherished lofty artistic ambitions, as far as one can judge from the voluminous output of its potteries. The richly molded pottery and the decorated pavement tiles perpetuated, throughout the seventeenth century, types already prevalent in the preceding century. Among these we may mention a decoration with blue foliage sketchily drawn, enlivened with touches of yellow and green, and birds and busts that appear on floor tiles discovered in the former Capuchin Convent and elsewhere. The local ceramic art developed in other directions also. From an inventory of movable goods, drawn up in 1624, on the death of the powerful Prince of Butera, we find reference to plates and bowls of white ware "gilded," and of a salt-cellar of "clay of Caltagirone gilded," besides details of Spanish pottery, all of which might have been made some years before.

FIG. *xli*

Research in the archives has shown that the art of the seventeenth century was flourishing and remunerative, in spite of untoward circumstances, such as the disappearance of the Gagini (which restricted the building activity of the city and consequently that of the tile makers) and the oppressive taxes. The potters had their own confraternity, which, between 1575 and 1676, used to meet in a little church in their own quarter of the city, dedicated to St. Agatha. Both the image and the initials of St. Agatha are found, painted in a manner reminiscent of the *compendiario*, upon vases and bowls dating from the late seventeenth century.

The violent earthquake that struck Eastern Sicily on January 11, 1693, considerably reduced the possibilities of documentation of activity before that date, and this event closes this period. The recovery, after the disaster, was slow and difficult.

The account of the development of ceramics in Sicily has thrown light on the island's relations with Liguria. At Palermo the merchant Giovanni Bramé, of Genoese origin, imported vases from Faenza in 1546. At Sciacca, Maxarato's great frieze adorned the Chapel of St. George of the Genoese. It was these Genoese who maintained important and continual trade links with Sciacca. At Caltagirone were working members of the famous Gagini family, sculptors and architects, one branch of which flourished in Liguria. The two regions were closely bound together by the same widely diffused interest in panels and ceramic wall or floor coverings, probably suggested by similar climatic conditions and by the common source of inspiration—Moorish and Christian Spain.

Liguria, like other Italian regions, possessed an ancient ceramic tradition, strengthened and refined by contacts with neighboring Tuscany and more distant Spain, which her merchants and navigators visited. The potters' art here in Liguria was immensely encouraged by the influx of artists from other centers, such as the Marches and the Romagna, especially during the sixteenth century, by her economic wealth, and perhaps by the hope of easy emigration to France and Spain. In fact, as we have already seen, Gian Francesco Pesaro arrived in Lyons from Genoa and obtained privileges in 1554, and Gambini and Tardessir, other *émigrés* from Genoa, received further privileges twenty years later.

Evidence of ceramist activity in Genoa is provided, from the fourteenth century, by examples of pottery that do not seem to differ noticeably from those of Tuscany and, in the fifteenth century and the beginning of the sixteenth, by vessels covered with slip and sgraffito. Particularly characteristic are the *laggioni*, or large tiles for pavements and walls, with geometric decoration in relief, on blue, green, yellow, orange, blackish-purple, and white enamel, or painted on a flat, smooth ground with typical arabesque and, later on, grotesque motifs. This art flourished in the late sixteenth century but declined in the early seventeenth.

Genoa seems to have owed her sixteenth-century vitality to immigrant potters, and especially to the workshop that Francesco da Pesaro had set up in 1528, at first in partnership with Francesco da Camerino, evidently induced to do so by the contacts established between Genoa and the Duchy of Urbino, with the accession to this dukedom of a Ligurian, Francesco Maria della Rovere, the nephew of Julius II.

The pottery workshop of Francesco da Pesaro, in which were trained his sons Tomaso, Cristoforo, and Gian Francesco, who all afterward emigrated to Seville and to Lyons, was very active; we hear of large orders being executed there toward the middle of the century. The type of ware produced showed the influence of models from other centers, from Venice, from the Romagna, and from overseas, thus proving the collaboration of artists of different regions and the possibilities afforded by contacts with the Near East. These FIG. *xlvi* vessels are adorned with coiled sprays of Damascene inspiration, painted in a threadlike dark blue on lavender-gray enamel, framing medallions containing busts or heraldic arms with touches of polychrome, foliage, and arabesques, "which are more used in Venice and Genoa than in other places," writes Piccolpasso. A master trained in the Faventine-Pelliparian school must have been responsible for the wonderful panels with St. George and St. John the Baptist in the Botto Chapel, FIG. *xlvii* erected in 1524 in the Church of S. Maria di Castello.

The Genoese ceramic production tended to use characteristic faintly tinted enamels in blue tones, thus anticipating, as a result of the opportunities afforded by maritime contacts, the seventeenth-century revolution in the use of color. At the end of the sixteenth century and the beginning of the seventeenth, the Pesaro workshop closed down and the Genoese production gradually ceased, yielding to the increasing productivity of Savona and Albisola.

The direct heir of this Genoese style seems to have been Savona, which boasted a guild of potters referred to in fourteenth-century statutes, which was reorganized in 1577 and 1613. Here in the closing years of the sixteenth century appeared, beside the masters of the *Arte Grossa* (the art of making hollow vessels), the far less numerous but more sophisticated masters of the *Arte Sottile* (the art of making shallow vessels, or flat tiles, etc.). Before this, in the fifteenth century and earlier still, Savona did not differ from Genoa, producing also painted and sgraffito pottery and, above all, *laggioni*.

In 1485 we find a record of the supply of 40,000 *laggioni*, in monochrome, white, green, and black, some with the heraldic arms of Pope Sixtus IV, made by the Tuscan artist Giovanni Nico for the Magnifico Paride Fieschi. From the entrance hall of the Palazzo Pavesi of Savona came the great sixteenth-century panels, the remains of a larger scheme, now at the Museo Civico in Turin and the Museo Artistico Industriale of Rome, with the figures of Marcellus and Scipio painted on a ground decorated with arabesques and an interlacing of circles and squares, which to some extent recall the framework of the panels in the Church of S. Maria di Castello in Genoa. Of a rather earlier date, that is, a date between that of the above-mentioned Genoese panels and that of the two from the Palazzo Pavesi, is the panel with the Madonna della Sapienza, dated 1529, formerly in the Palazzo del Carretto at Finalmarina, now in the Museo Civico of Genoa and also that with the magnificent St. Barbara, also at the Museo Civico of Turin.

Compared with the polychrome figured panels of the first half of the sixteenth century, which developed out of the production of tiles in the Spanish style, used for the adornment of public and private buildings in Savona, Genoa, and other places in Liguria and elsewhere, Savona could not produce, during the sixteenth century, pottery of any distinctive character. Such pottery does appear, however, and very decisively, toward the end of the century and during the following centuries, and exerted so powerful an influence as to initiate a movement that was to spread throughout Europe. The Ligurian majolica, together with that of Castelli, constitutes one of the most important original forms of Italian majolica in the seventeenth and early eighteenth centuries (the other important form being the white ware already described, which flourished throughout the seventeenth century) and had qualities that contributed greatly to its widespread popularity. This was undoubtedly due, to a great extent, to the immigration of artisans who naturally brought with them models and repertories of design. But there were other causes, among them the adoption of the blue palette inspired by the Oriental models of the late Ming style and, later on, of the Ch'ing style, whose influence Liguria was one of the first Western regions to feel. There was also the peculiar aptness of the new color scheme for use in vessels of Baroque design, which, by a natural evolution of taste and through the influence exercised by immigrant Faventine artists and their works, were enriched with a thick covering of brilliant enamel and with designs in which the sensitive *compendiario* style seemed allied to the ornate manner of wall decoration.

The Oriental influence, which was to become predominant in European ceramic art in the seventeenth century through the agency of the Dutch markets and workshops, was manifested in Savona in a decorative scheme with animals, insects, and figures, sometimes with vague reference to a hunting scene or reminiscent of a myth, in a vegetation rich in tufts of long-leaved plants—a design based on some Ming patterns that, in their turn, show the influence of Middle Eastern types, now considered to be the originals that inspired all the Chinese decorative schemes.

This form of decoration, attractive for its novelty, was not exclusive to Liguria but was characteristic of and widely applied to plates and large dishes, drugpots, spouted jars, and pharmacy amphoras, which were small quad-

xlvi

xlvii

xlviii

xlvi PHARMACY VASES WITH ORNAMENTATION INSPIRED BY MIDDLE EASTERN MODELS. GENOA (LATE 16TH CENT.). GENOA, NINO FERRARI COLL.
xlvii PANEL WITH ST. GEORGE. GENOA OR ALBISOLA (CA. 1530). GENOA, CHURCH OF S. MARIA DI CASTELLO, BOTTO CHAPEL. *xlviii* PLATE WITH MYTHOLOGICAL "CONVERSATION." SAVONA, STYLE OF GUIDOBONO (LATE 17TH CENT.). GENOA, C. BECKER COLL.

xlix

l

li

lii

xlix PHARMACY AMPHORA WITH "CALLIGRAPHIC" DECORATION. SAVONA (1619). GENOA, CAVANNA PHARMACY. *l* PHARMACY AMPHORA WITH "CALLIGRAPHIC" DECORATION. SAVONA (1619). GENOA, CAVANNA PHARMACY. *li* PLATE WITH IMMACULATE CONCEPTION. ANGARANO, MANARDI FACTORY (LATE 17TH CENT.). FAENZA MUSEUM. *lii* PLATE WITH SGRAFFITO FOLIAGE. PAVIA, ANTONIO MARIA CUZIO (17TH CENT.). PAVIA, MUSEO MALASPINA.

rangular flasks similar to Venetian glass shapes, also of Eastern inspiration. This ornamentation is sometimes, in both early and late examples, in polychrome, but it is generally painted with an intense blue outline, with the background a lighter blue on the covering white enamel. Grosso and Morazzoni call this manner *quasi calligrafica*, alluding to the careful accuracy, like that of the patient work of calligraphy, with which the outlines are drawn, in the same unvaried thickness, and to its faithful adherence to its models. Superb examples of this style, which may be dated 1619 and later, FIGS. *xlix, l* are seen in the vessels of the Cavanna pharmacy in Genoa, which came from the Grosso workshop.

The other type of seventeenth-century Savona pottery is represented by products of local artists, inspired by the cartoons and sometimes executed with the personal assistance of Genoese painters, such as Antonio Semino (to whom is attributed the fine panel with the Adoration of the Magi, in the Nino Ferrari Collection at Genoa), Bernardo, Valerio and G. Andrea Castello, Teramo Piaggio, Luca Cambiaso, and, later on, Domenico Piola, Gregorio De Ferrari, Lorenzo Tavarone, and Tavella.

The forms, vessels, and plates for display and use at the table and the amphoras, inspired by the most daring Baroque fantasy, with their potbellied form and fantastically shaped feet and necks, are cast with relief and intaglio decoration, frequently inspired by the moldings and *repoussé* of metallic prototypes. Harpies, shells, medallions with scrolled frames, gadrooning, fluting, and, under the influence of white ware, openwork baskets make up the vocabulary of ornament on pieces further enriched with applied masks and handles and spouts in the form of monsters or serpents, or with the heads of dogs, lions, or griffins. These dishes or pots are painted in various shades of blue, with religious or secular compositions directly traceable to the *compendiario*. In fact, they reflect the zestful spirit of the *compendiario*

in their buxom women, sumptuously attired with generous *décolleté* or with uncovered bosoms, in their knights on prancing steeds, in the typical mythological scenes with land- FIG. *xlviii* scape background, in the winged *amorini*, frequently arranged in pairs, in the marine deities, and in the figures of saints.

This kind of decoration, often inscribed with the lantern mark of the Chiodo workshop, was greatly if not decisively influenced in the second half of the seventeenth century by the Guidobono family. Giovan Antonio Guidobono was to leave the Chiodo pottery and start a workshop of his own and later to emigrate to Turin, to the Court of the Duke of Savoy, where he died in 1685. Other members of the family were Nicolò, Domenico, and Giovan Bartolomeo. Although the Guidobonos, and particularly the "Genoese priest" Giovan Bartolomeo, did ceramic work along with fresco and easel painting, according to their father's instructions, and frequently left Savona, the workshop continued to flourish, as is proved by the mark of the castle with the initials A.G., the arms of Savona with the initials B.G., the eagle with the sun and the ducal cap that distinguish their works, which were widely imitated.

The Guidobonos were responsible for the vessels supplied in 1666 to the pharmacy of the Ospedale di S. Paolo at Savona. The image of the Saint, painted upon a ground scattered with flowering sprays among which appear minor images, sketchily drawn, is painted with such a harmony of color and enamel and such graceful lines as to make this series the most perfect example of the Guidobono type. The style, carried on above all by Valente, although with heightened contrasts, was accompanied in the eighteenth century (which period is outside the scope of this treatise) by the polychrome fantasies of G. Agostino Ratti, who, like Giovan Antonio Guidobono more than fifty years earlier, was to introduce another most powerful innovation into the Savona potteries.

Albisola, which was to show such marked

originality during the eighteenth century, with the polychrome models of Andrea and Luigi Levantino, which seemed at first inspired by the art of Agostino Ratti, had produced during the two preceding centuries ware indistinguishable from that of Genoa and, later, of Savona. It must have been active in the sixteenth century, as the potters' guild drew up its statutes in 1589, as Savona had done before. Morazzoni tentatively ascribes to Albisola a drugpot with polychrome grotesques framing panels with heroic episodes from Roman history, clearly inspired by models from the Romagna; the already mentioned panels of the Botto Chapel at Genoa; and the Madonna della Sapienza, dated 1529, formerly at Finalmarina. In this he is probably influenced by the resemblance to two later panels, the one dated 1554 with a long inscription and a figured initial, painted by Gian Giacomo Sciacarama for the hospital of Albisola Superiore, and the other dated 1576 with the Adoration of the Shepherds, after an altarpiece by Semino, crowded with figures, painted by a Girolamo da Urbino for the Oratory of St. Anthony of Padua and now in the sacristy of the Church of Nostra Signora della Concordia in Albisola Marina.

In the seventeenth century, Albisola, which was producing considerable quantities of much-admired pottery for general utilitarian purposes, also began to make certain models decorated with little figures, flowers, and foliage of Oriental inspiration and Baroque scenes with figures after the style of the Guidobonos, already known in Savona. This provoked more dissension with the masters of Savona, whom they seemed to be imitating (sometimes even appearing to counterfeit their marks) and from whose overpowering influence they had to defend themselves.

The numerous workshops directed, at the end of the sixteenth century, by families whose names are famous in the history of Ligurian majolica—Salamone, Corradi, Grosso, Saetone, Sciacarama, Seirullo, and later on the Pescettos and the Bellottos—sent their products even to Genoa, where in 1676 the Ospedale del Pammatone ordered from Girolamo Meriga of Albisola Superiore an abundant supply of painted vases.

The craftsmen of Albisola were also largely responsible for the establishment or development of workshops on both sides of the Alps. Giovan Battista Seirullo was in Parma from 1583 to 1594; anonymous masters were at Mantua until 1630; Nicola Corradi was in Turin in 1649.

In Lyons, where, as we have seen, Italian masters had long been established, we find, in the second half of the sixteenth century, Bernardo and Filippo and other members of the Saetone family, who, with other craftsmen from Albisola, won renown there and acquired citizenship. To Nevers in 1565, summoned by Luigi Gonzaga of Mantua who had married Henriette de Clèves, came Domenico Corradi, who, aided by his brothers, acquired privileges, wealth, and honors. In 1578 he was naturalized and in 1604 he was raised to the ranks of the nobility. Twenty years after Domenico's arrival, Agostino Corradi also came to Nevers on the invitation of glassworkers, originally from Altare, and together they founded a new workshop which was to undergo various vicissitudes. To the work of these Corradi, Nevers owes its typical hunting scenes and "stories" after compositions by Antonio Tempesta, painted in dark blue, or dark blue and manganese brown, and occasionally in polychrome. The Corradi also introduced the fashion for decoration with flowers, animals, and insects scattered in varied patterns, which had been so popular in Savona.

In the Veneto a workshop was founded in 1670 by the brothers Ottaviano, Zorzi, and Sforza Manardi at Angarano, near Bassano. Baroni has attributed to this workshop some plates for display, gadrooned and molded in a style recalling the "white ware" of Faenza, adorned with foliage and animals in the so-called "calligraphic," or precise, style, known

The Veneto in the late 17th century

70

FIG. *li*

in the workshops of Savona and here executed in polychrome. The same pottery was probably responsible for the Baroque plates, panels, and vases, sometimes with large medallions bordered with foliage enclosing sacred images and scenes with figures, which reveal a special fondness for landscapes, architecture, and ruins, treated in polychrome, frequently in somewhat subdued tones, azure blue, violet, pale green, yellow, upon a pearly enamel known as *latesino*. These examples were formerly ascribed to the ceramic production of the Bertolini brothers, glassworkers, who were in Murano from 1753 on. The work of this pottery in the seventeenth century prepared the way for the workshop that Gian Battista Antonibon established later on at Nove, a few miles away from Bassano. It was in this pottery that Antonibon worked, from 1730 on. Inheriting the industry from Giovan Antonio Caffo and his Roman collaborators, Bartolomeo and Antonio Terchi, the last directors of the languishing workshop of the Manardi, Antonibon produced artistic pottery, which, during the course of the century and under the direction of his son Pasquale, achieved considerable variety and wealth of form and ornamentation. The latter was chiefly of a floral type and demo great

perfection in the enameling and in the workmanship, so that he won for this small center well-deserved renown and a highly honorable position.

The faïence with a slip coating beneath the glaze, with or without sgraffito decoration, of which we have already spoken, was much used for popular and utilitarian purposes because of the less costly character of its ingredients and the greater simplicity of its workmanship. Pavia, largely through the influence and the assistance of Antonio Maria Cuzio, a dignitary of the church, seems to have specialized in this kind of ware. Cuzio did a great deal to encourage it and was an amateur producer himself, as is proved by the inscription *Presbyter Antonius Maria Cutius Papiensis prothonotarius Apostolicus Fecit* (The priest Antonio Maria Cuzio, Papal Apostolic prothonotary, made it) on a plate at the Victoria and Albert Museum. Works marked with the name of Cuzio and of others of his family, written on the scrolls that frame the central design of plates dated between 1676 and 1694, decorated with tiny leaves, under a tawny brown or, less often, a green glaze, are among the last worthy manifestations of this ancient ceramic art.

FIG. *lii*

BIBLIOGRAPHY

The bibliography for Italian majolica is vast. The present list includes only recent and fundamental works on the subject, which in their turn contain more detailed bibliographies. For the same reason all articles in periodicals are omitted no matter how useful they may be in shedding light on the personality of an artist or the activities of a factory.

VANZOLINI, GIULIANO: *Istorie delle Fabbriche di Majoliche Metaurensi e delle attinenti ad esse raccolte a cura di G. V.* Vol. I contains articles by PASSERI on the majolicas of Pesaro, PUNGILEONI on those of Urbino, RAFFAELLI on those of Urbania, with notes and addenda. Vol. II contains articles by RANGHIASCI BRANCALEONI on Gubbio, MARCOALDI on Fabriano, CAMPORI on Ferrara, Turin, Mantua, Sassuolo, Modena, Reggio, Scandiano, S. Possidonio, Parma, with appendix. Pesaro, 1879.

MALAGOLA, CARLO: *Memorie storiche sulle maioliche di Faenza.* Bologna, 1880.

ARGNANI, FEDERICO: *Le ceramiche e maioliche faentine.* Faenza, 1889.

ARGNANI, FEDERICO: *Il Rinascimento delle ceramiche maiolicate in Faenza.* Text and plates. Faenza, 1898.

GUASTI, GAETANO: *Di Cafaggiolo e di altre fabbriche di ceramiche in Toscana.* Florence, 1902.

ARGNANI, FEDERICO: *Ceramiche e maioliche arcaiche faentine.* Faenza, 1903.

FALKE, OTTO VON: *Majolika.* Berlin, 1907.

BODE, WILHELM VON: *Die Anfänge der Majolikakunst in Toskana.* Berlin, 1911.

Faenza: Rivista di studi ceramici, Bollettino del Museo internazionale delle ceramiche di Faenza. Founded by GAETANO BALLARDINI. From 1913 onward.

FALKE, OTTO VON: *Die Majolikasammlung Alfred Pringsheim in München.* Leyden, 1914.

DE MAURI, LUIGI: *Le maioliche di Deruta.* Milan, 1924.

HANNOVER, EMIL: *Pottery and Porcelain. A Handbook for Collectors. I. Europe and the Near East: Earthenware and Stoneware.* Edited with notes and appendixes by BERNARD RACKHAM. London, 1925.

RACKHAM, BERNARD: *V.A.M. Guide to Italian maiolica.* London, 1933.

BALLARDINI, GAETANO: *Le ceramiche di Faenza.* Rome, L'Arte per tutti, 1933.

BALLARDINI, GAETANO: *Corpus della maiolica italiana. I. Le maioliche datate fino al 1530.* Rome, 1933.

BALLARDINI, GAETANO: "Maiolica," *Enciclopedia Italiana.* Rome, 1934.

BARONI, COSTANTINO: *Ceramiche italiane minori del Castello Sforzesco.* Milan, 1934.

PICCOLPASSO, CAV. CIPRIANO (of Casteldurante): *Li tre libri dell'arte del vasaio (The three books of the potter's art).* With translation and an introduction by BERNARD RACKHAM and ALBERT VAN DE PUT. London, V.A.M., 1934.

LIVERANI, GIUSEPPE: *Catalogo delle porcellane dei Medici.* Faenza, 1936.

BUSCAROLI, REZIO: *Rapporti di gusto e influssi di stile fra la pittura e la ceramica faentina del Quattrocento.* Faenza, 1937.

GRIGIONI, CARLO: *La bottega del vasaio del bel tempo.* Faenza, 1937.

BALLARDINI, GAETANO: *La maiolica italiana (dalle origini alla fine del Cinquecento).* Florence, N.E.M.I., 1938.

BALLARDINI, GAETANO: *Corpus della maiolica italiana. II. Le maioliche datate dal 1531 al 1535.* Rome, 1938.

LAMA, MELISANDA: *Il libro dei conti di un maiolicaro del Quattrocento (La vacchetta di Maestro Gentile Fornarini).* Faenza, 1939.

LIVERANI, GIUSEPPE, and GRIGIONI, CARLO: *L'officina maiolicara cinquecentesca dei Bergantini.* Faenza, 1939.

GROSSO, ORLANDO: *Mostra dell'antica maiolica ligure dal secolo XIV al secolo XVIII, Palazzo reale di Genova. Aprile-giugno 1939.* Genoa, 1939.

LANE, ARTHUR: *V.A.M. Guide to the Collection of Tiles.* London, 1939.

RACKHAM, BERNARD: *V.A.M. Catalogue of Italian Maiolica. I. Text. II. Plates.* London, 1940.

CONTON, LUIGI: *Le antiche ceramiche veneziane scoperte nella laguna.* Venice, 1940.

HONEY, WILLIAM BOWYER: *The Art of the Potter.* London, 1946.

LANE, ARTHUR: *Style in Pottery.* Oxford, 1948.

CHOMPRET, DR. J.: *Répertoire de la majolique italienne.* Preface by M. Pierre Verlet. Vol. I. Text. Vol. II. Plates. Paris, 1949.

POLIDORI, GIANCARLO: *La maiolica antica abruzzese.* Milan, 1949.

Morazzoni, Giuseppe: *La maiolica antica ligure*. Milan, 1951.

Honey, William Bowyer: *European Ceramic Art from the End of the Middle Ages to About 1815*. I. *Illustrated Historical Survey*. London, 1949. II. *A Dictionary*. London, 1952.

Rackham, Bernard: *Italian Maiolica*. London, 1952.

Polidori, Gian Carlo: *Studi artistici urbinati II*. Urbino, 1953.

Russo, Perez Guido: *Catalogo ragionato della raccolta Russo Perez di maioliche siciliane di proprietà della regione siciliana*. Palermo, 1954.

Vacca, Nicola: *La ceramica salentina*. Lecce, 1954.

Morazzoni, Giuseppe: *La maiolica antica veneta*. I. Milan, 1955.

Ragona, Nino: *La ceramica siciliana dalle origini ai nostri giorni*. Palermo, 1955.

The Visitation, center of plate
Faenza (1513)

Faenza Museum

PLATES

Plate 1

Faventine jugs and *panata* (jug with applied spout) from Orvieto
Archaic period (13th–14th cent.)

Faenza Museum

Plate 2

Jugs from Orvieto and Faenza; *panata* (jug with applied spout) from Umbria
Archaic period (13th–14th cent.)

Faenza Museum

Plate 3

Archaic jug with griffin
Siena (13th or 14th cent.)

Florence, Bargello

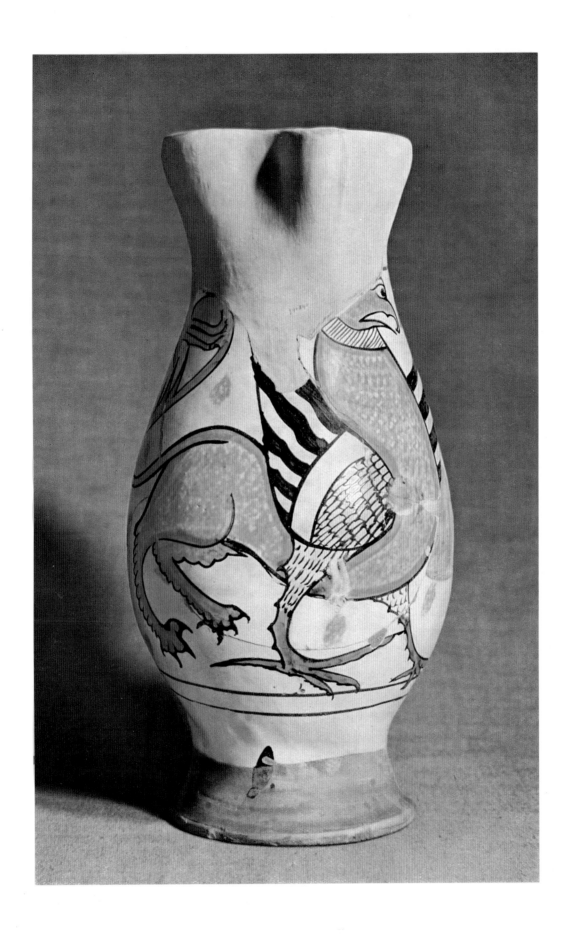

Plate 4

Two-handled jar with bust of man on twig, plastic relief
Orvieto (14th cent.)

Paris, Louvre

Plate 5

Two-handled jar with birds and oak leaves, in relief
Tuscan (mid-15th cent.)

Florence, Bargello

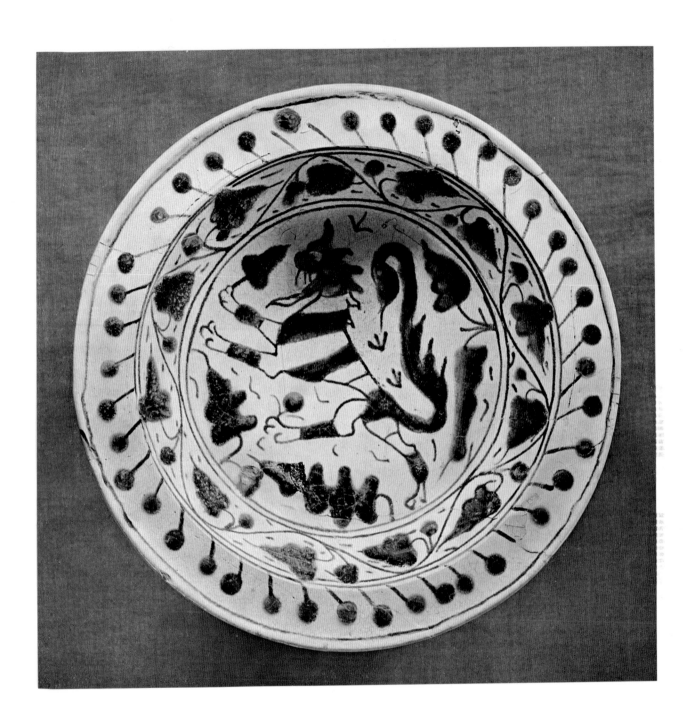

Plate 6
Plate with heraldic lion, leaves, and berries, in relief
Faenza (mid-15th cent.)
Faenza Museum

Plate 7
Italo-Moresque plate with Medici arms
Tuscan (mid-15th cent.)

Florence, Bargello

Plate 8
Plate with allegory of Love, brim decorated with "peacock feather" motif
Faenza (second half of 15th cent.)
London, Victoria and Albert Museum

Plate 9

a) Pharmacy jar with heraldic arms and decorative band of "peacock feather" motif
Faenza (second half of 15th cent.)

b) Jug with St. Bernardino's Sacred Initials: IHS
Faenza (late 15th cent.)

London, Victoria and Albert Museum

Plate 10

Pharmacy drugpot with "peacock feather" motif
Faenza (ca. 1480)

Milan, Giovanni Bolognesi Coll.

Plate 11
Pillbox with lid, decorated with Persian palmette motif
Faenza (late 15th cent.)
Faenza Museum

Plate 13

a) Bowl on foot, b) plate, with sgraffito decoration over slip
Ferrara or Bologna (second half of 15th cent.)

Paris, Louvre

Plate 14

Plate with sgraffito decoration over slip
Padua or Venice (late 15th cent.)

London, Victoria and Albert Museum

Plate 15
Enameled plastic group of patron saints of city of Bologna
Faenza (late 15th cent.)
Bologna, Museo Civico

Plate 16

Venus, Juno, and Minerva, detail of inkstand with Judgment of Paris
Faenza (1505)

Faenza Museum

Plate 17
Nativity
Faenza (late 15th or early 16th cent.)
Faenza Museum

Plate 18
Bust of old woman
Faenza (late 15th or early 16th cent.)
Cambridge, Fitzwilliam Museum

Plate 19
Dish with fruit
Faenza (first half of 16th cent.)
Faenza Museum

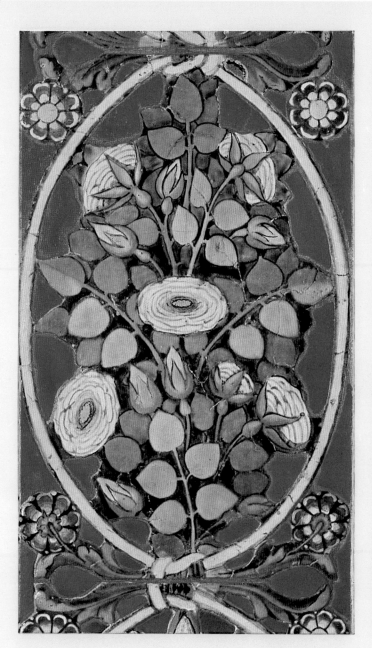

Plate 20
Tomb of Bishop Benozzo Federighi, detail of frame with majolica mosaic
Luca della Robbia (1455)
Florence, Church of S. Trinita

Plate 21
Tomb of Bishop Benozzo Federighi, detail of frame with majolica mosaic
Luca della Robbia (1455)
Florence, Church of S. Trinita

Plate 22

Female bust
Andrea della Robbia (1470–80)
Florence, Bargello

Plate 23

Medallion with heraldic arms of Ceppo
Giovanni della Robbia and others (1525–27)

Pistoia, Ospedale del Ceppo

Plate 24
Frieze with Works of Mercy: Finding Lodging for Pilgrims
Santi Viviani (1526–28)
Pistoia, Ospedale del Ceppo

Plate 25
Frieze with Works of Mercy: Visiting the Sick
Santi Viviani (1526–28)
Pistoia, Ospedale del Ceppo

Plate 26
Frieze with Works of Mercy: Visiting the Prisoners
Santi Viviani (1526–28)
Pistoia, Ospedale del Ceppo

Plate 27
Frieze with Works of Mercy: Feeding the Hungry
Santi Viviani (1526–28)
Pistoia, Ospedale del Ceppo

Plate 28
Plate with episode from Holy League against Charles VIII
Faenza (ca. 1495)
Cambridge, Fitzwilliam Museum

Plate 29
Plate with bust of "Giulia Bella"
Faenza (1490–1500)
Faenza Museum

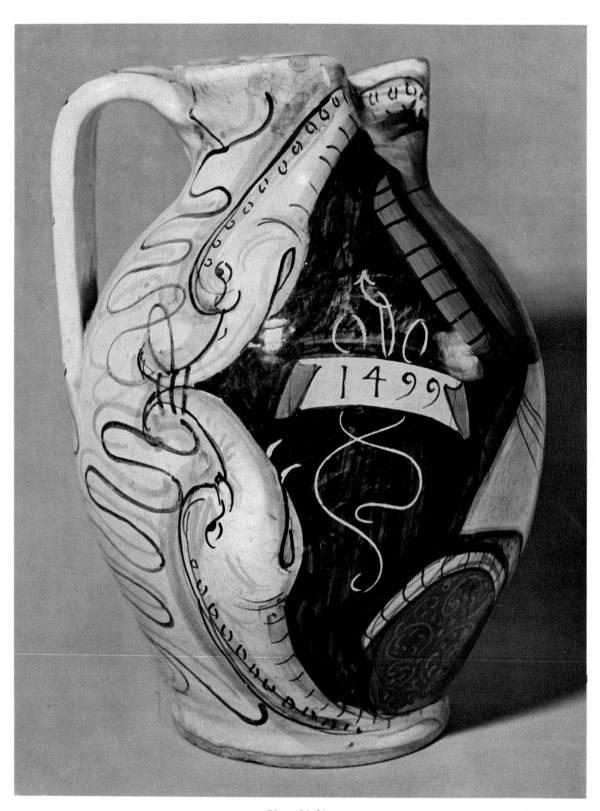

Plates 30–31
Jug with female bust
Faenza (1499)

Bologna, Museo Civico

Plate 32
Pharmacy jar with bust and lettering
Faenza (ca. 1500)
Faenza Museum

Plate 33

Plate with Perseus and Andromeda
Faenza, Monogrammist C.I. (1500–10)
London, Victoria and Albert Museum

Plate 34

Bowl with Hercules, grotesque border
Faenza (1500–10)

Faenza Museum

Plate 35

Panel with Resurrection
Faenza, Master of the Resurrection (ca. 1510)

London, Victoria and Albert Museum

Plate 36
Panel with Martyrdom of St. Sebastian
Faenza, Master of the Resurrection (ca. 1510)
Florence, Bargello

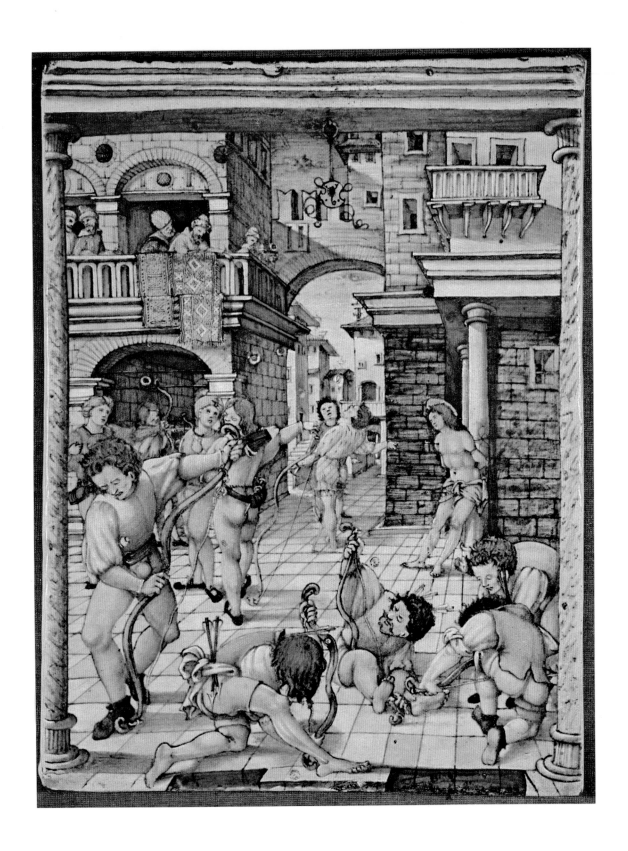

Plate 37

Plate with Christ among the Doctors and trophies
Master of the Resurrection, "In the workshop of Master Jero da Forlì" (ca. 1510)

London, Victoria and Albert Museum

Plate 38

Large plate with allegory
Faenza or Cafaggiolo (1515–20)

Cambridge, Fitzwilliam Museum

Plate 39
Large plate with episodes of Martyrdom and Resurrection of Christ
Deruta (1500–10)
Ravenna, Museo Nazionale

Plate 40
Plate with allegory of Love and trophies
Deruta (1510)
Paris, Louvre

Plate 41
Vase in shape of pine cone, metallic gold luster
Deruta (1510–20)
Florence, Bargello

Plate 42

Detail of pavement formerly in Church of S. Francesco at Deruta
Deruta (1524)

Deruta, Museo Civico

Plate 43
Large round "naveled" dish, lustered; with episode of Bradamante and Atlante from *Orlando Furioso*
Deruta, "The Friar" (1545)
London, Victoria and Albert Museum

Plate 44
Roundel with Judith and her Handmaid
Cafaggiolo, Jacopo (ca. 1510)
London, Victoria and Albert Museum

Plate 45

Plate with majolica artist
Cafaggiolo (ca. 1510)

London, Victoria and Albert Museum

Plate 46
Large plate with Leda and grotesques
Cafaggiolo (ca. 1515)
London, Victoria and Albert Museum

Plate 47
Bowl with School of Athens
Faenza, Master of Bergantini Bowl (1524)
Arezzo, Museo Civico

Plate 48
Plate with Aeneas and Dido
Faenza, Monogrammist F.R. (ca. 1525)
London, Victoria and Albert Museum

Plate 49
Bowl with Hercules and Deianira, lustered
Faenza, Monogrammist F.R. (1528)
Arezzo, Museo Civico

Plate 50

Bowl with Death of Lucretia
Faenza, Monogrammist F.R. (ca. 1530)

Plate 51
Plate with Medici-Strozzi arms and festoon
Faenza, Casa Pirota (ca. 1530)
London, Victoria and Albert Museum

Plate 52
Crespina with Orpheus and foliage decoration
Faenza (1530–35)
Faenza Museum

Plate 53
Crespina with Holy Friar, decorated in compartments
Faenza (1530–35)
Milan, Giovanni Bolognesi Coll.

Plate 54
Bowl with Resurrection of Christ
Faenza, Baldassare Manara (1535)
London, Victoria and Albert Museum

Plate 55

Plate from service for Isabella d'Este Gonzaga: Birth of Adonis
Nicola Pellipario (ca. 1519)

Bologna, Museo Civico

Plate 56
a) Bowl from service for Isabella d'Este Gonzaga: Abimelech observing Isaac and Rebecca
b) Bowl with Triumph of Death
Nicola Pellipario (ca. 1519)
Paris, Louvre

Plate 57

Large plate with Presentation of Virgin in Temple
Nicola Pellipario, Master Giorgio da Gubbio (1532)

Bologna, Museo Civico

Plate 58
Bowl with bust of "Fair Lady"
Imitator of Pellipario; lustered at Gubbio (1525–30)
Private coll.

Plate 59
Trencher with heraldic device and trophies
Casteldurante (1529)

Pesaro, Museo Civico

Plate 60
Pharmacy jar with Galatea and trophies
Casteldurante (ca. 1550)
Faenza Museum

Plate 61

Flattened bottle with trophy decoration
Casteldurante (1541)

Arezzo, Museo Civico

Plate 62
Bowl with Virgin, Jesus, and infant St. John Baptist (fragment)
Casteldurante (1525)
Arezzo, Museo Civico

Plate 63

Bowl with Phyllis and Aristotle
Casteldurante, Ippolito Rombaldotti (after 1636)

Faenza Museum

Plate 64

Large plate with Chastity of Joseph
Urbino, Francesco Xanto Avelli (1530–35)

FELIX QUI POTUIT GRAVIS TERRE ROMPERE
VINCULA

Florence, Bargello

Plate 65

Trencher with "story" of Pyramus and Thisbe
Urbino, Francesco Xanto Avelli (1535)

Bologna, Museo Civico

Plate 66
Roundel with Three Graces
Style of Casteldurante, lustered by Master Giorgio da Gubbio (1525)
London, Victoria and Albert Museum

Plate 67

Bowl with St. Jude

Casteldurante, Nicola Pellipario, lustered by Master Giorgio da Gubbio (1525)

Pesaro, Museo Civico

Plate 68
Nuptial bowl with lustered decoration in relief
Gubbio (ca. 1530)
Florence, Bargello

Plate 69
Large dish from service for Duke of Urbino; "stories" and Raphaelesque decoration
Urbino, Workshop of Orazio Fontana (1565–71)
Florence, Bargello

Plate 70
Wine cooler from service for Duke of Urbino, with Raphaelesque decoration
Urbino, Workshop of Orazio Fontana (1565–71)
Florence, Bargello

Plate 71

Plastic group: betrothed pair at table
Urbino (second half of 16th cent.)

Pesaro, Museo Civico

Plate 72

Inkstand with *Pietà*, made for Cardinal Baronio
Urbino, Patanazzi workshop (late 16th cent.)

Faenza Museum

Plate 73
Bowl with Fall of Man
Rimini (ca. 1535)
Paris, Louvre

Plate 74
Basin with allegory
Forlì (1562)
Ravenna, Museo Nazionale

Plate 75
Plate with mask and fruit, *berettino* enamel
Venice, Workshop of Master Domenico (ca. 1550)
London, Victoria and Albert Museum

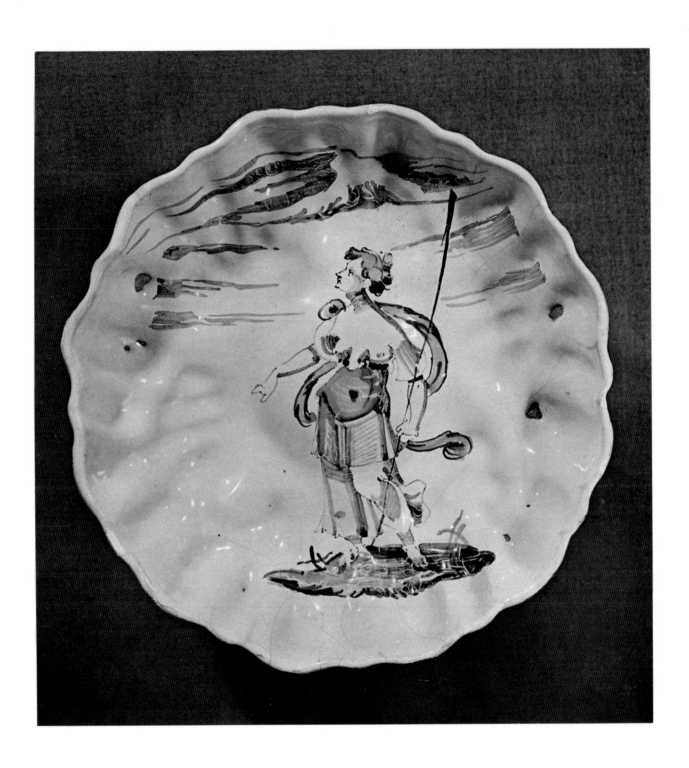

Plate 76
Crespina, compendiario style, with maiden holding spear
Faenza (1550–60)

Faenza Museum

Plate 77

Small panel, *compendiario* style, with Virgin and Child
Faenza, Battista Mazzanti (1602)

Faenza Museum

Plate 78

White ware: ornamental obelisks with heraldic arms and large dish
Faenza (ca. 1636)

Faenza Museum

Plate 79
Dropper and plate, *compendiario* style, lapis lazuli blue enamel
Faenza style (early 17th cent.)
Faenza Museum

Plate 80

Large jug with female bust
Montelupo (late 16th cent.)

Faenza Museum

Plate 81

Plate with musician
Montelupo (early 17th cent.)

Florence, Bargello

Plate 82
Plate with horses
Montelupo (early 17th cent.)
Florence, Bargello

Plate 83
Pharmacy jar decorated with trophies
Palermo (late 16th or early 17th cent.)
Faenza Museum

INDEXES

INDEX OF ARTISTS, WORKSHOPS, AND POTTERIES

INDEX OF OBJECTS, PLACES, PERSONS,
AND SUBJECTS

COLLECTIONS

253

ILLUSTRATIONS

BLACK-AND-WHITE ILLUSTRATIONS IN TEXT

Fig.

Fig.

ILLUSTRATIONS IN COLOR

Plate

6   Plate with heraldic lion, leaves, and berries, in relief. Faenza (mid-15th cent.). Faenza Museum.

7   Italo-Moresque plate with Medici arms. Tuscan (mid-15th cent.). Florence, Bargello.

8   Plate with allegory of Love, brim decorated with "peacock feather" motif. Faenza (second half of 15th cent.). London, Victoria and Albert Museum.

9   a) Pharmacy jar with heraldic arms and decorative band of "peacock feather" motif. Faenza (second half of 15th cent.). b) Jug with St. Bernardino's Sacred Initials: IHS. Faenza (late 15th cent.). London, Victoria and Albert Museum.

10   Pharmacy drugpot with "peacock feather" motif. Faenza (ca. 1480). Milan, Giovanni Bolognesi Coll.

11   Pillbox with lid, decorated with Persian palmette or pomegranate motif. Faenza (late 15th cent.). Faenza Museum.

12   Detail of pavement of Vaselli or St. Sebastian Chapel. Faenza (1487). Bologna, Church of S. Petronio.

13   a) Bowl on foot, b) plate, with sgraffito decoration over slip. Ferrara or Bologna (second half of 15th cent.). Paris, Louvre.

14   Plate with sgraffito decoration over slip. Padua or Venice (late 15th cent.). London, Victoria and Albert Museum.

15   Enameled plastic group of patron saints of city of Bologna. Faenza (late 15th cent.). Bologna, Museo Civico.

16   Venus, Juno, and Minerva, detail of inkstand with Judgment of Paris. Faenza (1505). Faenza Museum.

17   Nativity. Faenza (late 15th or early 16th cent.). Faenza Museum.

18   Bust of old woman. Faenza (late 15th or early 16th cent.). Cambridge, Fitzwilliam Museum.

19   Dish with fruit. Faenza (first half of 16th cent.). Faenza Museum.

20   Tomb of Bishop Benozzo Federighi, detail of frame with majolica mosaic. Luca della Robbia (1455). Florence, Church of S. Trinita.

21   Tomb of Bishop Benozzo Federighi, detail of frame with majolica mosaic, Luca della Robbia (1455). Florence, Church of S. Trinita.

22   Female bust. Andrea della Robbia (1470–80). Florence, Bargello.

23   Medallion with heraldic arms of Ceppo. Giovanni della Robbia and others (1525–27). Pistoia, Ospedale del Ceppo.

24   Frieze with Works of Mercy: Finding Lodging for Pilgrims. Santi Viviani (1526–28). Pistoia, Ospedale del Ceppo.

25   Frieze with Works of Mercy: Visiting the Sick. Santi Viviani (1526–28). Pistoia, Ospedale del Ceppo.

26   Frieze with Works of Mercy: Visiting the Prisoners. Santi Viviani (1526–28). Pistoia, Ospedale del Ceppo.

27   Frieze with Works of Mercy: Feeding the Hungry. Santi Viviani (1526–28). Pistoia, Ospedale del Ceppo.

28   Plate with episode from Holy League against Charles VIII. Faenza (ca. 1495). Cambridge, Fitzwillian Museum.

29   Plate with bust of "Giulia Bella." Faenza (1490–1500). Faenza Museum.

30-31   Jug with female bust. Faenza (1499). Bologna, Museo Civico.

32   Pharmacy jar with bust and lettering. Faenza (ca. 1500). Faenza Museum.

33   Plate with Perseus and Andromeda. Faenza, Monogrammist C.I. (1500–10). London, Victoria and Albert Museum.

34   Bowl with Hercules, grotesque border. Faenza (1500–10). Faenza Museum.

35   Panel with Resurrection. Faenza, Master of the Resurrection (ca. 1510). London, Victoria and Albert Museum.

36   Panel with Martyrdom of St. Sebastian. Faenza, Master of the Resurrection (ca. 1510). Florence, Bargello.

37   Plate with Christ among the Doctors, and trophies. Master of the Resurrection, "In the workshop of Master Jero da Forlì" (ca. 1510). London, Victoria and Albert Museum.

38   Large plate with allegory. Faenza or Cafaggiolo (1515–20). Cambridge, Fitzwilliam Museum.

39   Large plate with episodes of Martyrdom and Resurrection of Christ. Deruta (1500–10). Ravenna, Museo Nazionale.

40   Plate with allegory of Love, and trophies. Deruta (1510). Paris, Louvre.

41   Vase in shape of pine cone, metallic gold luster. Deruta (1510–20). Florence, Bargello.

42   Detail of pavement formerly in Church of S. Francesco at Deruta. Deruta (1524). Deruta, Museo Civico.

43   Large round "naveled" dish, lustered; with episode of Bradamante and Atlante from *Orlando Furioso*. Deruta, "The Friar" (1545). London, Victoria and Albert Museum.

44   Roundel with Judith and her Handmaid. Cafaggiolo, Jacopo (ca. 1510). London, Victoria and Albert Museum.

45   Plate with majolica artist. Cafaggiolo (ca. 1510). London, Victoria and Albert Museum.

46   Large plate with Leda and grotesques. Cafaggiolo (ca. 1515). London, Victoria and Albert Museum.

47   Bowl with School of Athens. Faenza, Master of Bergantini Bowl (1524). Arezzo, Museo Civico.

48   Plate with Aeneas and Dido. Faenza, Monogrammist F.R. (ca. 1525). London, Victoria and Albert Museum.

49   Bowl with Hercules and Deianira, lustered. Faenza, Monogrammist F.R. (1528). Arezzo, Museo Civico.

50   Bowl with Death of Lucretia. Faenza, Monogrammist F.R. (ca. 1530). London, Victoria and Albert Museum.

257

PHOTOGRAPHIC CREDITS

Alinari, Florence: *ix, x*

Ashmolean Museum, Oxford: *xxxv*

Boymans Museum, Rotterdam: *xxxii*

British Museum, London: *xxiii, xxiv, xxvi, xxvii, xxxiii, xxxiv*

Direction Générale des Monuments Historiques, Paris: *v*

Foto Borchi, Faenza: *iii, xi, xviii, xxxvii, xxxix, xl, li*

Foto F. Briganti: *xlii*

Foto G. Chiolini, Pavia: *ii*

Foto Cresta, Genoa: *xlvi, xlvii, xlviii, xlix, l*

Foto Di Paolo, Teramo: *xliii*

Foto Fiorentini, Venice: *xxxi, xxxvi*

Foto Giuliani, Faenza: *xxviii*

Foto Porta, Milan: *xii*

Foto Ragona, Caltagirone: *iv*

Ugolino Della Gherardesca, Bolgheri: *xiii*

Istituto Artigianato Ceramica, Caltagirone: *xli*

Kunstindustrimuseum, Copenhagen: *vii*

Municipal Museum, The Hague: *viii*

Museo Civico, Bologna: *xix, xx, xxix*

Museo Civico, Pavia: *lii*

Museo Internazionale delle Ceramiche, Faenza: *i*

Sovrintendenza Gallerie, Florence: *xxi, xxii, xxv, xxx*

Sovrintendenza Gallerie, Naples: *xliv, xlv*

Victoria and Albert Museum, London: *vi, xiv, xv, xvi, xvii, xxxviii*

All the colored photographs are the property of Electa Editrice S.p.A., Milan.

The publishers and the author wish to express their gratitude to the directors of museums and to the owners of collections whose kind collaboration has made possible the photographic reproduction in this book of objects in their custody.

THE FIRST ITALIAN EDITION OF THIS VOLUME
WAS PUBLISHED UNDER THE AUSPICES OF THE
BANCA NAZIONALE DEL LAVORO

Printed April 30, 1960, in Milan

COLLABORATORS

CARTIERA VENTURA, CARTIERA BURGO, ZINCOGRAFIA
ALTIMANI, S.A.E.S., STABILIMENTO GRAFICO MARIETTI,
ARTI GRAFICHE MILANESI, LEGATORIA TORRIANI

THE COLOR REPRODUCTIONS WERE MADE EXPRESSLY
FOR ELECTA EDITRICE BY "ARTE E COLORE," THE STUDIO
DORVYNE, AND FINE ART ENGRAVERS